This Man
TRUMAN

PRESIDENT HARRY S. TRUMAN

This Man TRUMAN

by

FRANK McNAUGHTON

and

WALTER HEHMEYER

Whittlesey House

McGRAW-HILL BOOK COMPANY, INC.

New York   *London*

THIS MAN TRUMAN

Copyright, 1945, *by* McGraw-Hill Book Company, Inc.

E
814
·M3

2/65

*This book is produced in full compliance
with the government's regulations for conserving paper and other essential materials.*

First Printing

96134

PUBLISHED BY WHITTLESEY HOUSE
A division of the McGraw-Hill Book Company, Inc.

Printed in the United States of America

"I ask only to be a good and
faithful servant of my Lord
and my people."

Harry S. Truman

Contents

This Man
TRUMAN

Chapter One

The Family

THERE WAS NO PARTICULAR CELEBRATION ON MAY 8, 1884, in the little town of Lamar, Barton County, western Missouri, north of the lead mining center of Joplin.

Word went up and down the street that the Trumans had a baby—a boy who kicked and squalled lustily and seemed to be singularly unmarked by destiny for anything greater than a life behind the plow or behind the counters of some crossroads store.

The first-born was promptly named Harry S., after a bachelor uncle, Harrison Young, the S. standing for nothing in particular. It was merely an initial adopted because it stood for each of the grandfathers: Anderson Shippe Truman and Solomon Young. In later years, the boy was to prefer the name Shippe, but the initial never bore other than nameless significance.

This birth in Lamar, Missouri, was perhaps not an inauspicious start for a future president of the United States. But the fact that Harry Truman arrived in the White House after sixty-one years is eloquent testimony to the miracle of the American government which reaches down into obscure hamlets to raise up men from the sinews of the people.

Lamar in 1884 was a pretty little village of some eight hundred souls. Its streets were rutted by wagons and buggies which the hill folk of the Ozarks, simple, sometimes ignorant but deeply sincere people, drove into town every Saturday to buy salt, pepper, sugar, calico, perhaps a bit of candy, and a few other essentials of life.

This is rolling country and its hills rise around a rugged, rambling terrain of deep and verdant green, furred over with stout oak, exquisitely beautiful and restful when mantled by the rainy mists that brush and scour along their tops. Life radiates from the post office in such hamlets, or from the grocery store, or the county fair. For it is at such places that the farmers and the townfolk gather to discuss crops, the local news, visits, births, deaths, and cracker-barrel politics. There is nothing here of grandness or classicism. The dance is still predominantly the old-fashioned square. The musical instruments are a piano for sounding chords, a "fiddle" for carrying the melody and, perhaps, an occasional guitar. Still favorite tunes are the old stand-bys like the "Irish Washerwoman," "Turkey in the Straw," and the ever-loved "Missouri Waltz."

The town is laid out in square blocks. The houses are mostly frame structures inelegantly built and deeply pitted and browned by the lashing rains and thunderstorms that sweep through the foothills. In May, this country is at its best, with spring crowding winter gently away, the grass

The Family

greening beneath the freshet showers, the brooks plentifully supplied with perch, and flowers coming into full blossom.

This is not a dramatic country; rather a country of quiet hills and of simple folk who know and think not a great deal of the world outside. Some of them say "poke" for bag, "kin" for can, "hit" for it, and "injun" for engine. They discuss the crops and the local society but seldom indulge in high politics or world theories. Theirs is a lot circumscribed by their restful hills, the intensity of grubbing out an existence, and the joys and woes of their neighbors whom they know intimately and love generously. It is rural America, the northern edge of the Ozarks where, as has been said, the people "shingle the roof with a bullhide and use the tail for a lightning rod."

Most of the farms are small, forty and fifty and a hundred acres, devoted to pasture, hay, and some corn for "winter feeding." The ever-elemental question is, "How is your corn crop this year?"

Both sides of the Truman family fitted into these rural simple surroundings. Yet by all standards they were comfortably fixed, and the Young branch of the family might even be said to have been well off.

Anderson Shippe Truman, the paternal grandfather, and his wife, Mary Jane Holmes Truman, arrived in western Missouri, then a comparative frontier, at about the same time the maternal grandfather, Solomon Young, and his wife, Harriet Louise Gregg Young, freighted their belongings and traveled by river boat down the Ohio, up the

The Family

Mississippi, then up the Missouri, finally establishing themselves at old Westport Landing, near Independence, Missouri, the eastern terminus of the wagon freight routes to the romantic West.

This was in the early 1840's and both families had come to Missouri from Shelby County, Kentucky. There is a story, often told about the Trumans of Kentucky, that Nancy Tyler Holmes, the President's great-grandmother, was scalped by Indians. As the savage's blade cut around her hairline, she lay absolutely motionless, knowing that the slightest movement indicating she was still alive would mean instant death. Thereafter, she always wore a covering to hide her glabrous and scarred head.

Anderson Truman settled on a farm in Jackson County that lay in the vicinity of what is now Thirty-ninth and Indiana Streets, Kansas City; and John Anderson Truman, their son and father of the President, was born there in 1851.

Grandfather Solomon Young set up an ox-team wagon freight from Westport Landing to Salt Lake City, thence to San Francisco. The venture prospered and Grandfather Young saved sufficient money to purchase five thousand acres in Jackson County, seventeen miles south of Westport Landing. As his wagon freight business prospered, Solomon Young kept investing in land and at one time he owned some Negro slaves and was a man of recognized means in west central Missouri. While he ran his wagon trains, often making the long, tortuous journey to Salt Lake City by him-

The Family

self and then out to San Francisco, Grandmother Harriet Young looked after the farms and kept affairs in order. In 1868 Grandfather Young purchased six hundred acres near Grandview in Jackson County. There was no better land in all the state, and the soil was unmarked by plow and un-sapped by tillage and perennial crops. It cost $30 an acre. Earlier in 1854 he had also acquired a ranch in the vicinity of Sacramento, California, but the family never lived there.

While Grandfather Young was amassing considerable means, the Trumans were meeting with more modest cir-cumstances. Grandfather Anderson Truman sold the farm in what is now Kansas City and moved with his family to Platte County, Missouri, farmed there for a few years and then returned to Jackson County and bought another farm of 160 acres east of Holmes Park Village, only three miles from the Solomon Young farm at Grandview.

It was in these western Missouri hills near the Kansas border, that the Truman family, and the Youngs, fiercely Democratic and staunch Confederates, lived through the war between the states, and it is an ignorant man indeed from this countryside who cannot recount almost endlessly the misadventures of the Civil War. They recall Quantrill's Guerrillas and Jim Lane, who carried fire and pistol along the Kansas-Missouri border.

Redheaded Grandmother Harriet Young, whom Harry Truman always recalls as "a grand old lady with the most beautiful hair I've ever seen," was also a woman who "stood for no foolishness." She gave alms freely, bore nine children of whom seven lived to maturity, cared for numerous slave children, neighbor orphans, and in her spare time raised two nephews. As a young housewife, she had experienced directly the horrors of guerrilla warfare.

Early one gray morning in 1861 while Grandfather Young was away in California, Jim Lane, the ruthless leader of the Union-sympathizing Kansas "Red Legs," rode into the yard at the farmhouse and ordered Harriet Young to make biscuits for his motley crew of raiders. She began mixing dough, fired up the kitchen stove, quieted the children and then began baking. She baked biscuits until her fingers blistered, while outside shots rang out and the hogs in the pens squealed as the marauders invaded the barnyard. After a hearty breakfast, the Lane raiders hacked hams from the four hundred hogs they had butchered, slung them across their saddles, set the barns on fire, and then rode away. After sacking the Young farmstead, Lane and his men raided Osceola on the Osage River, pillaging and looting the town, and killing some twenty inhabitants.

In reprisal for such raids as these, bands of Missouri robbers would ride into Kansas. Each side committed outrages against the other with many innocent people being murdered. The climax of this internecine warfare came in the summer of 1863 when Quantrill staged his famous raid on Lawrence, Kansas. Leading a band of nearly five hundred men, he rode into the town at daybreak with the intention of burning every house and killing every man. They rode

The Family

through the streets, robbing and burning and shooting every man on sight, nearly two hundred in all.

The drastic Order Number 11 issued by the Union General Thomas Ewing followed the wanton attack on Lawrence. Almost all residents in Jackson, Cass, and Bates Counties in Missouri were ordered to leave their homes. They had to move out of the counties or to military posts. Grain and hay had to be yielded up to the military authorities.

The war years of 1861-1865 inflicted grievous wounds upon Missouri because the state was divided. She was both slave and free though virtually surrounded on three sides by states fighting for the Union cause.

Missouri sent 109,111 men into the Union armies and another 30,000 wore the gray—including William Young, an uncle of Harry Truman who served as a foot soldier in General Sterling Price's army. Truman's father was too young to serve. No other member of the immediate family joined the colors, but they were Confederate Democrats by conviction, believing they had enlisted in the cause of patriotism and independence and were fighting for the sacred right of self-determination.

There were few large plantation owners in Missouri although 115,000 slaves were owned in the state in 1860. The Confederate sympathizers were determined to preserve their agrarian economy and the institutions surrounding it, though most Confederates did not themselves own slaves. The whole weight of military might, economic strength, and geographical position in Missouri favored the North. The Federal Government had more and better trained soldiers who were able to prevent Confederate armies in the north and south of Missouri from joining. Moreover, Northern leaders were more resourceful and far-sighted. And most of all, the Federal Government possessed vastly greater resources of wealth and industry.

Missouri did not witness great battles during the Civil War, but the fighting was bitter and tragic. Families were torn apart as sons and brothers joined opposing armies. Friendly neighbors became sworn enemies—it was a cruel, ugly struggle of burning, pillaging, murder, injustice, bushwhacking and guerrilla engagements.

In spite of its superiority, the Union side never gained complete control of the state. General Price's men raided deep into the Union lines, alarming and hounding the Federal troops. There were bloody clashes at Booneville and at Wilson's Creek near Lamar where Harry Truman was born, and along the Blue and Big Blue Rivers where, many years later, he was to play as a boy. Stiff fighting was also seen at Westport Landing where Grandfather Young harnessed his wagon trains.

The Civil War left deep stains in the state. For months after hostilities had ceased, bandits and guerrilla bands continued their depredations, and peace was slow in coming. It was hard to reform after years of lawlessness. Bandits like Jesse James and his brother Frank, who had served under Quantrill during the war, carried on their plunder and robbing to give Missouri the reputation of the "bandit state" for decades to come.

But the riches and abundance of the opened frontier in the West had closed up the wounds of war by the time Harry Truman was born twenty years later.

John Truman and Martha Ellen Young were neighborhood sweethearts and grew up together on their families' neighboring farms at Grandview and Holmes Park Village. When the couple were married, they moved to Lamar, where John established a fairly successful business of buying horses and mules. They lived in a low, white frame house, the President's birthplace, which still stands. The Truman mule and horse barn was a sort of gathering place for farm folk who wanted to gossip, talk Democratic politics, or arrange a horse trade, for John Truman was always ready to "swing a deal." He bought and sold dozens of animals every week and was, as his sons recall, "the kind of a man who never passed a cow but what he stopped and tried to buy her." It was not a flourishing business, but one that sometimes turned a handsome profit, produced a fair living by Missouri standards but not a great deal more. Missourians are by nature sharp traders, unsentimental and proud of giving the other fellow a "skinning." John Truman learned this the practical way; but since he was also a farmer who had known nothing but horses, mules and cows, he managed to do his fair share of the "skinning" and remain solvent.

The Family

St. Louis, Missouri, then as now, was the horse and mule market of the entire country, and the animals John Truman bought and did not resell to local farmers he peddled to the buyers who came from the city.

Only Harry S. was born to the Trumans at Lamar. A second boy, John Vivian, was born on April 25, 1886, on a farm at Harrisonville, Missouri. The third child, Mary Jane, was born to the family on August 12, 1889, at Grandview.

Longevity is quite usual in the family, though there have been some early deaths. Anderson Shippe Truman, the grandfather, lived to be seventy-one; his wife Mary Jane, for whom the President's daughter, Mary Margaret Truman, was named, died at fifty-seven. Grandfather Young passed away in his seventies, and Grandmother Young lived to be ninety-one. Harry Truman's only living aunt, Mrs. Joseph Tilford Noland of Independence, Missouri, celebrated her ninety-sixth birthday on May 6, 1945. Truman's father died at sixty-four. His mother is an indomitable, surprisingly vigorous woman of ninety-three.

When Harry Truman was about four years old, the Trumans moved into the white, rambling, eight-room, two-story farmhouse of Grandfather Solomon Young at Grandview. There were two big hay and stock barns, a giant-sized granary, and a half-dozen hogsheds, all painted white like the house. It was a thriving establishment, watered profusely by clear, cool springs that bubbled up from the soil.

The Family

There was an outdoor privy, some good Shorthorn and Hereford cattle, normally a couple of hundred head of hogs, and endless hard work. This farm may properly be said to be the beginning of Harry Truman's life. He remembers it intimately with a strong feeling of nostalgia, and he lived here until he was almost seven.

It was on the Young farm that he tagged along after his mother, then a woman in her middle thirties, while she gathered the eggs from under the clucking, protesting hens. He followed her as she picked strawberries, canned tomatoes, and performed all the endless farming chores.

He loved to carry the egg basket for his mother, to walk along with her as she gathered vegetables from the big garden, and to prod his toes into the black, coolly rich soil; to kick aside the weeds that withered almost instantly in the hot sun. He wore overalls, munched homemade sugar cookies, and liked to pull up the red radishes moist with earth, shine them on his overalls and bite into them so his tongue would sting.

He was like the people around him, undisturbed by matters of great pith and moment. He rambled through the yard seeking out birds' nests in the elm and box elder trees, finding a baby cottontail rabbit, watching the farm livestock, and admiring the sleek, butter-fat little pigs that squealed and scampered through the lots.

His mother, like Grandmother Young, was a strict disciplinarian and kept near at hand a slim switch or slipper with which to paddle her children. Harry Truman often said later, "We were taught that punishment always followed transgression, and my mother saw to it that it did." John Truman did not punish the children that way. He scolded them, but "that hurt worse than a good spanking."

On their wedding day in 1882, John Truman and his wife Martha posed for this old-fashioned photograph. Two years later when their first child, Harry S., was born in Lemar, the President's father was so elated that he nailed a muleshoe over the front door to bring his son good luck.

It was in this little Lemar, Missouri, house, with a shingle roof and white clapboards, that Harry S. Truman, Thirty-second President of the United States, was born on May 8, 1884. At the time of his birth, the house was unnumbered, and the street it was on had no name. Truman's father had built it two years before. Near by were the barns where the family mule- and horse-trading business was conducted.

Chapter Two

The Boy

I T WAS THE YEAR 1891 WHEN THE TRUMAN FAMILY moved on to Independence, Missouri, a larger town, where the father could better conduct his business of buying and selling animals. The family lived here in a square, frame house at Waldo Street and River Boulevard.

By this time the first mouldings of the character and the qualities of Harry Truman had begun. He was not a light-hearted child, nor was he given to pranks or mischief. He had started to read the Bible, not as most children read the Bible for its stories, but for as much as a boy's mind could catch of its deeper meaning, its moral lessons and great truths. It instilled in him a seriousness that became marked in a boy so young. He could quote many verses at random and in a childlike way he knew their beauty and could understand the allegorical significance. By the time he was ten he had read almost twice through the Bible. His eyes, in the meantime, had begun to develop a decided feebleness, due no doubt in part to his intensive reading habits as well as to a tendency toward optical difficulty.

At the age of eight, because of his weakened eyes, he began to wear the thick-lensed glasses he still requires. His parents delayed for two years his entrance into school, and he was going on nine when he entered grade school in Independence. But, once enrolled, his lessons became an absorbing interest with him, particularly history and most of all Civil War history, with mathematics and Latin as secondary subjects. In general, he was a fine student, a fact to which his instructors still bear witness. Within eight years, despite his late start, he had finished the Independence High School.

Ethel Noland, his cousin, attests to his studious nature. "Harry was a model boy, the favorite of all the relatives, but that didn't make other boys hate him," she says. "He studied hard, and his grade card, although I was a year ahead of him, used to make me ashamed of myself.

"He sometimes got into small mischief, and sometimes he quarreled with Vivian, and then mother Truman would switch them and make them behave. But everybody liked Harry, and he was so kind and friendly they just couldn't help it."

The sports and games which intrigue most boys of school age were lost on Harry Truman. He was frail physically, and his poor eyesight was a handicap in baseball, shinny—a rustic approximation of hockey—or other games. On afternoons, he could be found not on the baseball lots but at the Independence public library studying his lessons or reaching for books on the shelves.

By the time he was twelve, he had read a great many of the books in the local library, which stocked some four thousand volumes including the encyclopedias. As he has often said, "I had more useless information floating around in my head than any man." He had a retentive, acute memory, and the facts that he kept culling from biographies and history texts had a habit of sticking with him.

In some respects his could not be said to have been a normal boy's life. He never had a bicycle or many toys. He could not compete in sports because of his eyes. Moreover, his temperament was deeply studious and serious.

Unlike many other boys in rural Missouri, Harry Truman never wore overalls or dungarees to school. His mother always dressed him well and insisted that he wear a tie and clean shirt. On Sunday, he put on a neat dark suit with high lapels, and attended Sunday school at the First Presbyterian Church of Independence, though when he was eighteen he became a Baptist. He always knew his Scripture lesson and prided himself in his ability to recite the verses of the day.

In school and on the playground, he was the conciliator, developing early the ability to get along with all classes and shades of individuals without clash or conflict. When arguments arose or quarrels threatened, the serious, bespectacled little boy was first to suggest compromise, to talk peace, to urge a reconciliation, and to credit the sincerity of all groups of disputants. He hated a fight. It made him sick and seemed ignorant and brutish. As he was to say often in later years, "I'd always rather build a house than break a window," and "It was always a lot more fun when we got along than when we fought." Sometimes he quarreled with his brother, Vivian, but neither can recall fighting with other boys.

He became the semi-official mediator of school squabbles, a role that he enjoyed. But even in those days, Harry Truman would take his own stand, good-naturedly refusing to change his position once he believed it was right.

It was at the First Presbyterian Sunday school in Independence that he met a young, wavy-haired girl that Harry Truman thought was about the prettiest child he had ever seen.

As Harry Truman later described that meeting: "I met a very beautiful little girl with lovely blue eyes and the prettiest golden curls I have ever seen. She was my sweetheart and ideal when I was a little boy—and she still is!" Her name was Bess Wallace.

At ten, Truman and sister Mary Jane began to study music under Mrs. E. C. White of Kansas City. She was the wife of the principal of the Kansas City Central High School. Truman showed aptitude as a pupil, and though he did not display any unusual talent at the piano, he became quite proficient.

Harry Truman's musical education was strict and precise. Mrs. White rapped his knuckles with her pencil, insisted on precision and attention to the metronome. She took him quickly through the preliminary exercises and then instilled in him a love and feeling for classical music. He is one President who is a pianist in his own right and it is not wide of the truth to assert that the great White House concert grand piano will offer him many moments of relaxation and comfort in trying times.

Harry Truman is at ease at the piano and plays effortlessly and with relish. He does not play by ear. His mind is trained and accustomed to playing by note. His favorite pieces are Chopin's *Waltz in A flat,* Opus 42; Mozart's *Sonata IX for Piano,* and Beethoven's *Sonata in C minor* —the "Pathétique." He never misses, if he can help it, hearing a concert pianist, and he has listened to most everyone of any ability. He believes that the late Joseph Lhévinne, a Russian, is perhaps the greatest of all he has heard.

Even today he delights in playing duets with his only child, twenty-one-year-old Mary Margaret.

A few Biblical verses struck in Truman the same chord and the same depth of feeling that inclined his affection to the "Pathétique Sonata." He still recites these verses today, and with an understanding foreign to one ignorant of the real meaning of the Scriptures. One group of verses emphasizes the advance of age and decay, and is from Ecclesiastes XII:

In the day when the keepers of the house shall tremble, and the strong men shall bow themselves, and the grinders cease because they are few, and those that look out of the windows be darkened,

And the doors shall be shut in the streets, when the sound of the grinding is low, and he shall rise up at the voice of the bird, and all the daughters of musick shall be brought low. . . .

The Boy

. . . Then shall the dust return to the earth as it was: and the spirit shall return unto God who gave it.

Vanity of vanities, saith the preacher; all is vanity.

Another favorite verse is and long has been to Harry Truman a beacon light, a warning and a guide: *Woe unto you, when all men shall speak well of you! for so did their fathers to the false prophets.* (LUKE 6:26)

These precepts have been guiding principles in Truman's life. He learned the verses as a boy, and they have been, throughout his career, truths to which he could anchor himself and comforts to which he could repair in moments of difficulty and trouble. He also likes to quote from the twentieth chapter of Exodus, wherein Moses speaks of great moral precepts, and he reads often the Sermon on the Mount as recited in Matthew, chapters five, six and seven.

The Spanish-American War in 1898, when Truman was barely fourteen, fired the youth with an ambition to be a soldier. He and a group of his school classmates, who included Charles G. Ross, former correspondent of the *St. Louis Post-Dispatch*, who is now the White House press secretary, held weekly drills with .22-caliber rifles. They were getting ready but the war ended before they were old enough to serve or to know the real meaning of military training.

The drills frequently ended with fishing excursions on the Little Blue or Missouri Rivers. Occasionally they tramped the woods, shot a neighbor's chicken and roasted it in the protective covert of some grove. On the fishing trips, young Harry Truman seldom wet a hook or baited a worm. Instead, he took along a history or biography, lounged on the bank and read, offering advice or reading favorite paragraphs, often to the disgust of his carefree companions.

While he was in high school, Truman decided it was time to be earning his own money. He walked over to the drugstore on the northeast corner of the Independence square and asked Jim Clinton for a part-time job mornings and afternoons, and was hired. Clinton, now dead many years, was a businessman who was all business, and for the three dollars a week which he paid out, he intended and was determined to get full value and a considerable volume of work. Truman was to handle the soda fountain; was to open the store at six-thirty o'clock every morning, mop the floor, clean away the trash, polish up the jugs and bottles, and in his spare moments when not waiting on the trade, to wash and dry what looked like millions of bottles littering the cramped space behind the prescription counter. Truman worked a year at this part-time job, and he learned that money is hard to earn and must not be wasted.

One day Jim Clinton directed him to dust the entire stock of bottles. The boy took one look at the long rows of glass on the shelves and decided he had enough of this at three dollars a week. He yearned for a better job, and for several months he had thought of going to work for the *Kansas City Star*, an arch-Republican newspaper that circulated throughout Missouri, Kansas and Oklahoma. Here was opportunity, and Harry Truman grabbed at it.

He quit Jim Clinton, drew his three dollars for the last week's work, and then took his first and only venture into journalism.

The *Star* needed good boys, but not for editors or reporters. It needed boys to wrap the papers that flowed in a seemingly torrential avalanche from its grinding presses, and this was Harry Truman's job at seven dollars a week— more than double his former pay. He wrapped papers for six months, until he dreamed newspapers, was haunted by newspapers, and could see only the words, *Kansas City Star,* when he went to bed at night.

In 1901, when seventeen-year-old Harry Truman was graduated from Independence High School, father John Truman met financial reverses which swept away their home at Waldo Street and River Boulevard. It was clear that there would be no more money for education; there was barely enough left to purchase a house at 2108 Park Avenue, Kansas City, a less pretentious dwelling. It was necessary that the boys go to work.

It was in May of that same year, 1901, that Truman was given an appointment to West Point by Democratic Congressman William S. Cowherd. He was elated with this opportunity and readily imagined for himself a promising career in the Regular Army. He studied hard that summer in preparation for his entrance examinations. And in the fall he passed all the West Point tests—save one. When the

Harry Truman (right) at the age of four, with his brother John Vivian, then two years old. Vivian, who was named after a Confederate cavalry officer, still works on the farm at Grandview.

In the bottom row at extreme left, neatly dressed Harry Truman poses with his classmates of the second grade in grammar school at Independence. On the top step, by the crudely made door, the stern but kindly looking teacher watches over her brood of camera-conscious pupils.

doctors examined his eyes they found them to be weak and overstrained. He was rejected for this reason. It was one of the bitterest disappointments of his life.

Sadly Truman went to the L. J. Smith Construction Company, which was then building a trackage for the Santa Fe Railroad from Sheffield to Sibley, Missouri. He made application and got a job as timekeeper for the rough and crude construction crews at thirty-five dollars a month "and board." The foreman, Ed Smith, a brother of L. J., was a martinet who bossed three crews in as many camps. Most of the men were hoboes picked up in Kansas City or along the railroad, and some of them were common drunks. Harry Truman twice daily pumped a three-wheel handcar between the camps to check up on the crews and to make out their time tickets. The crews were paid twice monthly, and every other Saturday the slim, bespectacled boy sat in the back room of a saloon in Independence or Sheffield, Missouri, and there made out and signed the pay checks which were carried, in most cases, right around the partition to the bar and spent there for fifteen-cent shot whisky.

He lived in the tents that housed the crews, ate the chow that was served up in tin pans by company cooks, and in his own words learned "all the cusswords in the English language—not by ear but by note." It was a coarse and hard life, bitterly frank, deeply profane, and ruggedly realistic. Six months of it were enough. Harry Truman was tired of seeing shiftless, uncouth men work for two weeks, draw their pay and spend it in devastating drunkenness, then go back to work for more money only to repeat their drinking bouts on the next pay day. Truman took a week end off and went to Kansas City. He was then eighteen years old and wondering just what future a youth of such limited means, with what he felt was such limited intelligence and such circumscribed opportunity, might ever enjoy.

He had lived with the railroad crews, swapped towering and earthy oaths with them, roughed his hands on pick and shovel, and kept his time records with meticulous care. But this was no life for Harry Truman.

Brother Vivian had taken a position as a clerk at the National Bank of Commerce in Kansas City, and early that Monday morning Harry Truman, a callow and somewhat abashed youth, walked into the bank and asked for a job. He didn't much expect to get it. But he knew that he could keep books after a fashion and that he could add and subtract. He convinced the bank's officers that he could do the work and was hired to keep and post ledgers at exactly his Santa Fe salary of thirty-five dollars a month. "Board" was not included, but he lived at home.

Bank work was not easy. The clerks worked in a basement. The vice-president, Charles H. Moore, was the official disciplinarian, and as Truman recalled many years later, "he was an artist at it." It seemed that the bank's officers "would always remember a trivial mistake when a clerk asked for a raise" and find this sufficient reason for denying it for "raises were hard to get and if a man got an additional five dollars a month he was a go-getter."

The Boy

A year later Truman moved over to the Union National Bank of Kansas City as a bookkeeper at $60 a month and soon was making $125 a month, which admittedly was "a heck of a high salary." Harry Truman was going places. He stayed at this job for three years, until he was twenty-two, and saved his money. When in 1904 father Truman traded the home on Park Avenue for an equity in eighty acres of land near Clinton and went there to farm, Harry moved to a boarding house at 1314 Troost Avenue, and lived with a family named Trow. He lived on a budget, and often his lunches comprised a ten-cent pocket packet purchased at a street-side food stand.

Frequently he spent Sunday at the Wallace home in Independence to see Bess, or else he went down to Grandview to visit Grandmother Harriet Young and bachelor Uncle Harrison Young on the big farm.

One day Harrison Young told his nephew that he wanted to move into town and take life easy. He outlined a plan for John and Martha Truman, Harry and Vivian, to return to the Young farm, which they had left fifteen years before; renting out the little acreage John Truman had acquired near Clinton. Harry took the proposition to his father, who thought it was a good idea, if Harry and Vivian could help. They agreed, and in 1906 the Trumans moved back to the farm Harry as a boy had loved so well.

He was twenty-two, back in overalls and happy, and as convinced as only a youth can be that here he would spend the rest of his life. This was what he wanted.

Chapter Three

The Farmer

HARRY TRUMAN WAS A GOOD BANK CLERK. HE KEPT
his records neat, and he was honest and careful.
But he was a better farmer. When he left the
Union National Bank and returned to the farm with his
father and mother, Mary Jane and Vivian, and Grandmother Young, there followed ten of the happiest years of
his life. He was twenty-two and at the very age when
youths are most likely to sense the glamour and excitement
of nature's truths. The decade was saddened only by the
death of his father, John Truman, in 1915.

Truman has often said of those years on the farm, "I
wish I had kept a diary." He and his father managed the
farm together and worked together. Truman acquired then
the habit of early rising, 4:30 A.M. in the summers, and 6:30
A.M. in the winters, long before the sun had climbed clear
and warm over the Missouri prairie or pierced through the
snowy haze of January. This habit of early rising is still
with him. It will never leave him. And in his office as President of the United States it will afford opportunity to study
in the quiet of morning when faculties are refreshed and the
mind and body invigorated by the sound, undisturbed sleep

into which he slides easily and instantly upon hitting the pillow.

On the farm his was the job that raised sweat—salt sweat —and sent him in from the fields at sunset with his overalls grimed and caked with dust and grease and dirt. He learned "to plow as straight a furrow as could be found in all Missouri."

He liked to ride along on the Emerson gang plow, holding the levers with his hardened hands, while the earth curled in a black, sweetly fresh ribbon at the side of the shining steel moldboard. He learned to pull a neat left turn with the plow at the end of a furrow and bring the horses sharply around to start off at a right angle from the furrow he had just completed.

"Riding one of these plows all day, day after day," Truman often remarked later, "gives one time to think. I've settled all of the ills of mankind in one way or another riding along, seeing that each animal pulled his part of the load."

As on all Missouri farms, the hot sun shone in a coppered glare needed for ample growth of the corn and early ripening of the billowing stands of long-stem wheat. There were the breakfasts of eggs, ham, and biscuits and jelly; the dinners lush and rich from the garden, and the smell of cornbread baking in the oven; the suppers of steak or fried chicken. There stood the fattening cow rich with the pregnancy of life. Crows signaled nightfall as they flew in westerly procession to some roosting grove rasping out their last few harsh cries of the day. The chirp of the prairie sparrow was dry and parched in blistering hot weather. There was also the harvest of fall and the rough grating of shucking peg on dry husk and kernel.

Here was something deeper, something genuine and more fundamental than rows of figures between the red-ruled lines of a ledger page; something that reached out and gripped the heart. It was not like the debits and credits of notes or checks. This was life.

A pleasant discord sounded in the shrill grating of the old iron pump lifting from the deep well a water that never flowed through waterworks or chlorinating systems, and was not obtained by turning a spigot. It tasted clean and half frozen, and was pumped, on hot workdays, into the old stone jug wrapped in a burlap sack which itself was wet and in the sun gave up its moisture in an evaporative process that made the jug, indeed, a cooler—keeping the contents cold and fresh until late afternoon. Placed in the shade of a jimson weed or a gooseberry bush, the jug would be cool until evening, and refreshing throughout the long afternoons.

There were even musical notes in the sharp blows of clawhammer on staple, the pull of barbed and woven wire as Harry Truman stretched and stapled his fences to hold the hogs and cattle within the pastures of the farm. There was a pleasure in hewing out with pocketknife and drawknife the round wooden pegs called "cultivator pins," which kept the cultivator shovels in place, but conveniently broke and released the shovel when it struck a rock or stump. The best pegs, Truman learned, were made from hedge, that steely tough wood sometimes called bois d'arc. He used to smash up a common brickbat and with its sandy dust polish up the ploughshares and shovels so the soil would not cling to them. And he liked to see the metal take on a mirror polish and smoothness as the season's ploughing advanced.

There were the warm, rainy nights when the weather was ideally suited to the pigging sows, and on these nights Harry Truman kept vigil. He would gather up the fresh brood in a bushel basket or tin washtub lined with straw, while with his free hand he swung a club to ward off the enraged sow as he carried the new-born pigs to the haven and safety of the hogsheds. He still bears to this day the marks made by enraged and unreasoning sows which charged through his protective flail, to rip his overalls and legs with their champing jaws. No one who has not "carried pigs to the barn" can imagine the hazard of the task.

He learned to bang the No. 12 scoop against the corn-crib door and yell "whoo-e-e" to call the hogs from a quarter of a mile away, and to bellow "so-o boss" until the cows over the hill came galloping awkwardly to the barn, spilling droplets of milk from strained and distended udders. He learned to "juice" a cow in a matter of minutes, and listened for the first streams of milk to rattle into the tin pail, then watch the golden white fluid climb up in a heavy foam that would perch an inch or more above the pail.

Of evenings and in early morning he took his three-

The Farmer

legged rustic stool and sat down to milk both for the family table, and for the pig trough in a pen adjoining the barn lot. He learned early that the job of bucket feeding a weaning calf was both precarious and aggravating. It seemed that the calf before galloping away inevitably blew the last mouthful of sudsy milk out through its nostrils upon the feeder, or butted the bucket with its last quarts of milk into the holder's arms.

In summertime he would be patient when the flies were biting. They would spread over the cows in a cloud of black, as the animals switched viciously and slapped the milker with tails caked with mud or manure. He enjoyed as much as any farm youth to milk a stream into the mouth of a near-by cat, watch the animal lick its chops in surprised satisfaction and then start following up the sudden stream of nourishment to its source.

Truman loved this work. He could smell of the lush alfalfa and clover that fell in orderly, six-foot swaths over the sickle of his mower, the cool sweetness of the hay after it had been raked and dried and was ready for the barn. He wore his straw hat in summer and felt in winter. Both were battered and sometimes torn, and always greasy. His work gloves softened only a little the calluses that were rough and thick in his palms. In the rolled cuffs of his overalls he gathered a daily load of black dirt, hayseed, straw, machine shop shavings, and grains that had to be emptied each night before entering the house.

Late in June, thundershowers would come up suddenly

This formal portrait of the President at the age of thirteen reveals an eager, friendly countenance. His lessons were an absorbing interest, and at school he often acted as conciliator of classroom disputes. Although his weak eyes prevented him from competing in sports, he liked to play with his friends down by the Big Blue River.

Grandfather Young's farm at Grandview, where Truman spent ten of the happiest years of his life. Sometimes he rested in the shade of the big maple trees and cooled off after a hot day of plowing in the fields. He left the farm to fight in France during World War I. When he returned, he tried to make plans so he could again be a Missouri farmer, but circumstances always seemed to interfere.

in a towering frown of black cloud, generally from the southwest, with blinding flashes of lightning and earsplitting volleys of thunder followed quickly by the cool, pelting dash of rain that rattled on the roof, flooded the barn lots, and soaked deep around the tap and brace roots of the corn. He learned that wind in the east or southeast meant rain, but when the wind was from the west or southwest it was safe to mow the hay.

As he plowed, he idly picked out the caricatures painted by the hot-weather cumulus clouds in heavenly billows of white along the horizon, piling up in giant stacks and often loosing white-hot ropes of lightning. He labored in the fields, and while he was resting he would heat the iron wagon tires and shrink them to the wooden wheels with geometric precision.

He learned the surgical art of castrating pigs and became such an expert that neighbors joked that "when Harry sharpens his knife the pigs run out to pasture." One afternoon as he drove the horses from the barn lot, a two-year-old whirled and kicked viciously as it ran through the gate. The hoof landed a glancing blow on Truman's left leg, below the knee. As soon as he could get back on his feet, he hobbled about his work. That evening when he started to separate a calf from the cow it had sucked, he grabbed the calf around the neck to wrestle it away, and threw his weight heavily on his left foot. The bone which had been cracked by the colt's kick earlier in the afternoon snapped, and he collapsed. It was a clean fracture about four inches below the knee, and it was weeks before he could work again. But his leg healed completely and he walks without a limp.

He liked to feel the snap of the traces as he hooked the horses into the singletrees, and he learned the art of juggling the two handles bolted to the beams of a cultivator, manipulating the shovels as he walked along so that a long mound of rich earth was thrown up around the young corn to protect and anchor the brace roots, and at the same time cover up the persistent weeds.

There were long Saturday evenings at Grandview and Belton stores, with talks of local politics—Democratic politics—crops and weather; the thrifty, frugal farmers shopped for foods the farm did not produce, and for dungarees, husking mittens for winter wear, and leather gloves for summer. The family traded mostly at Belton, for that town had a general store and a bank. Grandview had neither.

Winters were cold and bleak with heavy snows that in the sub-zero temperatures turned crisp and squeaked and squealed beneath the iron-shod wheels of wagon or buggy. Elm trees contracting in the cold would snap and crack like revolver shots. In such weather there was hay to be hauled from the stack to the cattle, and the early morning job of pulling comb and brush through the crackling, shaggy hair of the horses and mules.

On week ends, farmer Harry Truman boarded the train and rode twenty miles up to Independence to court Bess Wallace. Her family was one of considerable affluence, her grandfather, George Porterfield Gates, being a fairly well-to-do man, owning most of the Waggoner-Gates Milling business which still operates in Independence. Grandfather Gates died in June, 1918, while Truman was in France, but Grandmother Margaret Gates and the Wallaces continued to live in their big, rambling, sixteen-room frame house at 219 North Delaware Street, in those days a dwelling that aroused the admiration of neighbors for blocks around. It has now, as it had then, plain furnishings, a large farm-style kitchen, and a big yard studded with shade trees. Dave Wallace, Bess' father, was a lawyer of established ability in Independence, and the Gateses and Wallaces were among the recognized families of the community.

Harry Truman and Bess Wallace frequently attended church together, even though Truman had joined the Baptist Church and she was an Episcopalian. They were in school together and had graduated from grade and high school in the same classes. Each thought the other was pretty nice. Bess Wallace was the only girl Harry Truman ever loved though there were many rival suitors. Bess Wallace admittedly was a "catch" for any young man, and there was no lack of social callers at the Wallace home.

In 1913, Truman bought a dark, four-cylinder Stafford automobile, the thirteenth off the Stafford assembly floor in Kansas City, and then he called more often at the Wallace home. He and Bess Wallace sometimes attended church socials or box suppers, those curious rural auctions that supply money and raise jealousies in the name of local schools or charities. Neighbors noticed that Harry Truman always helped himself generously to the sandwiches, cake and pie boxed by Bess Wallace, and with her proudly ate its contents. He liked her cooking even as much, they remarked, as she seemed to like his company.

Money on the farm was not plentiful, and what there was of it was literally scratched and raked from the soil. Not that the soil was unwilling or niggardly, but prices were mediocre, work was backbreaking, and nature often ruined a carefully nurtured crop with hail, freezing, or the searing sun. Harry Truman learned to study and respect the whims of nature. He could forecast almost to the day when a cow would calve or a mare would foal.

It was a rare night when he did not complete his day's work with an hour or two of reading, for his education did not end with high school or his departure from Kansas City. He liked this life. He likes it yet and is perfectly at home talking cattle, discussing corn crops, or debating the merits of Poland China versus Duroc Jersey on a Missouri farm. These were lean, hard years, but in experience, in the formation of character and the fruition of understanding and true humility—which is the seed of all greatness—they were rich years. Truman not only learned to love the farm and its animals and its labors, but he loved to learn from it.

He learned to trim a horse's hooves with his pocketknife and to file a deep groove at right angles to the crack in a hoof to prevent laming the animal. He discovered the way to hitch a young colt with a heavier, gentler animal and thus break it to the mysteries and the slaveries of collar, hame,

The Farmer

and tug. He learned how to stick a cow for clover bloat—by thrusting deeply into the animal's abdomen with a long-bladed pocketknife, four ribs up from the rump, and there piercing the agonized, gas-inflated stomach which, properly lanced, healed almost miraculously.

He could compute accurately the number of bushels of corn in a crib by measuring its cubic contents, and figure the tons of hay in a stack by the same method. The *Daily Drovers' Telegram*, a market newspaper of large circulation, was read almost as religiously as he studied his Bible and *Plutarch's Lives*, for on the farm the hog and cattle market, the horse and mule trade were important and vital matters of everyday living. He read the *Kansas City Star* and studied politics, and once in 1912 when the Democratic convention was meeting at Baltimore and trying to choose between Champ Clark and Woodrow Wilson he tied his team to the fence, streaked to a telegraph station, and asked if the operator of that mysterious ticker had any knowledge of the man chosen as the Presidential nominee.

Truman studied the "horse doctor book" which is a part of every farm library, and was his own veterinarian, his own hired hand, his own bookkeeper and manager. He swung a scythe and mowed the weeds around the fence rows, nailed shingles on the barn, moved the privy, and performed all of the myriad chores that make farming an art as well as one of the most difficult occupations in the world.

Truman figured how to measure the acreage he had plowed by counting the revolutions of the cultivator

· 33 ·

wheel the length of one row, multiplying this figure by the number of rows plowed, and computing the area thus covered. After all, unless something like this were done to occupy one's mind, cultivating corn was a dull job. He and his father bought a new manure spreader, hauled manure from the farm barns and from adjoining towns to spread upon the fields, and followed a strict plan of crop rotation: from clover to corn to oats to wheat and then back to clover. The land improved in quality. Production of wheat increased from thirteen to nineteen bushels per acre. The field of corn increased from thirty-five to seventy bushels per acre. It was killing work but it paid fairly well.

Occasionally after dusk with the dishes washed and dried, the milk put in the cellar to cool, Harry Truman would sit at the piano and play the music of the masters, akin in many respects to the music of life all around him. His hands were hard and strong, and adept at the quick-motion lift-up that would splinter a hickory pitchfork handle in an instant against an overload of hay as he pitched up to his father on the stack. But his fingers did not lose their touch for the keyboard. He played well, sometimes just to rest his tired and weary body.

In December, 1909, he joined the Belton Masonic Lodge and was made a junior warden. As he plowed the fields, he delivered to the teams he drove the Masonic lectures he had learned by rote. He helped to organize the Grandview Masonic Lodge and was its first master. Later, in 1940, he was to be elected Grand Master of Missouri.

The Farmer

It was in early 1915 that his father first showed signs of the illness that was to bring on his death. This was a blow that shocked the entire family and took from Harry Truman one of his closest companions. The two had worked together in the fields, and while they pitched hay or plowed the corn they had talked long and deeply over life, politics, and all the countryside gossip. In the early summer of that year, father John Truman began to complain of pains in his stomach, and though he continued to do some work his face showed clearly that he suffered from a recurrent and painful misery. He finally went to bed, and on the doctor's advice, was moved to a Kansas City hospital for an operation. The exact nature of the ailment was never precisely settled. The operation was a serious one, but for a time thereafter, it seemed that he was getting better and he was taken home. But in October he suddenly grew much worse. In a few days he died, at the age of sixty-four. The family arranged his burial at the Forest Hills Cemetery in South Kansas City, and then went sadly back to the everyday routine of the farm.

Upon his father's death Truman was appointed to succeed him as road overseer in the southern half of Washington township, which job forced him to spend his spare time collecting taxes, fixing grades, and repairing culverts and bridges.

Truman's father had always taken an active part in local politics. For four years before his death, he had been road overseer for Washington Township, in which the Grandview farm was located. And from 1906 until he died, he had served as judge for elections in the Grandview precinct, his son Harry usually acting as clerk, a job that early whetted his interest in the political contests that stirred up the county, city, and nation. Succeeding his father as road overseer was Harry Truman's first political post.

He gave up the job when he disagreed with the county commissioners. They did not believe he should make so many improvements. Truman felt that he should. With the support of Congressman William P. Borland, a Democrat, Truman was then appointed postmaster at Grandview, a job that paid about fifty dollars a month. Truman hired as his assistant Ella Hall and let her run the office and take the money which in those years was sufficient to hire two men for farm labor. She needed the money more than he did. Truman gave her the entire salary.

Business reverses and borrowings in the lean years of the 1920's and early 1930's were to force the family to sell a part of the Grandview farm in order to clear up mortgages and settle the tangled legal business of an estate. At one time Jackson County held a $30,000 mortgage on part of the farm and subsequently sold the land, some of it back to the Trumans, for more than $40,000. Today the six hundred acres have shrunk to 340 acres, owned jointly by the President, sister Mary Jane, and brother Vivian. Vivian is the manager-operator of the farm and also assistant director of the Kansas City office of the Federal Housing Adminis-

Acme Photo

Picnics and hay rides were favorite pastimes in rural Missouri during Truman's youth. Here, wearing a bow tie, he sits (second from left), in a farm wagon. Often an outing would lead to Cave Spring, near Independence, where covered wagons once stopped for fresh water before heading further west over the prairies. Or they would visit the limestone ledges which served as fortifications during bloody guerrilla engagements of the Civil War.

Dressed in the blue of the Missouri Guard as a youth of twenty-two. It was the sight of this uniform that angered Truman's grandmother, prompting her to remind him of his family's Confederate background.

The Farmer

tration. As in the early days, the Truman family still buys and sells horses, mules, and hogs.

In his days on the farm, Harry Truman liked best the growing season, the summer with its heat and its flourishing growth of crops and weeds. On those nights when the air was slightly cool and he could hear the corn rustle in the soft brush of air, he sat on the front porch or along the fence and thought and wondered. He was not wondering about his future. The present was almost idyllic despite its hardness. As he rubbed the calluses on his hands, he was wondering, after nearly ten peaceful years on the farm, about war.

Chapter Four

The Soldier

TRUMAN REMEMBERED THE DAYS OF THE SPANISH-American War when as a lad of fourteen, he and other boys had drilled with .22-caliber rifles and had talked of Dewey at Manila and General Shafter in Cuba.

In 1905, while he was a bank clerk, Truman went to Kansas City, joined the National Guard and went religiously at his marching and drilling. On June 14—Flag Day—Captain George R. Collins organized a battery of light artillery. Truman became a charter member.

"After reading all the books I could obtain in the Independence and Kansas City public libraries on history and government from early Egypt to the United States of America," Truman said in explanation of this start of his military career, "I came to the conclusion that every citizen should know something about the military, finance or banking, and agriculture. All my heroes or great leaders were somewhat familiar with one or the other or all three."

In August of that year he had gone to his first encampment at Cape Girardeau, traveling by train to St. Louis, and thence by steamboat down the Mississippi River to the Cape. It was a great experience, and Truman liked the excitement and hard work of the camp. Thereafter for many years he regularly attended camps, and at Fort Riley, Kansas, was given a corporal's warrant. As a farmer he carried on his military training. He remembered visiting his Grandmother Harriet Young as a guardsman. The Young family had not even then forgotten the infamous Order No. 11 of 1863 which required them to leave their farm for a military post. And they also remembered that the family home had been pillaged and robbed by Jim Lane and his Union-sympathizing guerrilla troops.

Truman recalls vividly how Grandmother Harriet fixed him with a stern and withering look as he strode into her sitting room in his blue uniform. Her lips drew out into a white thin line and she spoke crisply:

"Harry! This is the first time a uniform of that color has been in this house since the Civil War. Don't bring it back!"

When another famous Missourian, General John J. Pershing of Laclede, was at the Mexican border in 1916 pursuing Pancho Villa, Harry Truman remained at home to care for the farm, his mind hardly less intent upon the invasion of Mexico than upon the flight and pursuit of Villa. He was then a member of Battery B of the Missouri National Guard, and when the United States entered the World War on April 6, 1917, Truman was made a first lieutenant.

In August he was sent for further training to Camp Doniphan near Fort Sill, Oklahoma, at the edge of the Wichita Mountains. It was here in the 1880's that the bloody

The Soldier

old Apache chief, Geronimo, had been detained and imprisoned after his capture by United States Army regiments. The fort was the largest and by far the best training ground for artillery, and Harry Truman liked it no less than the farm. But he was not a model soldier. He was criticized and reprimanded by his superiors for infractions of regulations that sprang more from lack of acquaintance than intent to commit breaches.

Truman was serving in Captain Pete Allen's Battery F but because of his knowledge of accountancy and the standard collection practices of banks, Colonel Karl D. Demm put Truman in charge of the regimental canteen, a business venture of some proportions. He did not attempt to handle the job alone, but instead called in a Jewish friend, Eddie Jacobson, and together the pair organized their canteen-store. They began by collecting a two-dollar investment from each of the 1,100 men. Jacobson, a sergeant and former shirt salesman at Kansas City, was put in charge of the canteen. Truman acted as overseer and policy-maker. Jacobson knew the rules of buying low and selling profitably, and within six months each man had received back his initial investment of two dollars, and managers Truman and Jacobson declared $15,000 in dividends on the original $2,200 investment.

Truman, meanwhile, was developing into one of the finest artillery officers in the camp. He had a flair for mathematics, and a faculty for calculating triangulation that surprised his instructors and elder officers. He did not attempt to explain it, just said drily, "The job is to hit the target, lay them down on it, isn't it?" He seemed to calculate his ranges by a sort of rule-of-thumb process but the shells landed on or near the targets. Truman learned most of his artillery technique from Lieutenant Colonel Robert M. Danford, author and authority on field fire. Truman progressed with such promise that he was raised to a captaincy, then picked with thirty-nine other officers and three hundred men and sent to France with the 129th Field Artillery of the 35th Division, Missouri and Kansas National Guard, an outfit that was destined to see much fighting and to sustain heavy casualties in the Argonne. Truman landed from a transport—the steamship "George Washington"—at Brest, France, on April 13, 1918, twenty-seven years to the day before he was to serve his first day as President of the United States.

Truman's contingent was sent to artillery schools at Chantillon-sur-Seine and Coetquidon, to learn the finer points of artillery fire from French line officers.

On July 11, 1918, Captain Truman was given command of Battery D, 129th Artillery, a rough outfit of Kansas City Irishmen utterly devoid of regard for shoulder bars, uninhibited in their treatment of officers, unafraid of war or the guardhouse, and proud of the five captains' scalps already hanging at their belts. Most of them were from DeLasalle High School and a few had attended Rockhurst College in Kansas City.

"I won't forget that day," Truman often said later. "I

was never so scared in my life. They had driven out five captains, and they were as tough a bunch of men as you will ever find. Each man was a fine soldier, but taken together the outfit was almost insufferable. They loved trouble. If they couldn't mix it with the Boche they were ready to mix it among themselves."

There were 188 men and 167 horses in Battery D. The men decided to initiate Truman into the outfit with conduct bordering on near rebellion. The horses were wild, unruly, and hard to manage. It was absurdly easy to have a runaway, scattering equipment and impedimenta along the French countryside. On Truman's first day in command of the battery, the men arranged for such a stampede and the ensuing scramble was manufactured with realism and authenticity. The men had envisaged Captain Harry Truman riding frantically by the side of the runaway, attempting to bring order out of the riot. They were wrong. Harry Truman not only had seen runaways in Missouri on the farm, but he himself had fought to bring frightened, terrorized animals under control. He knew this one was staged from the minute it started.

Captain Truman sat on his horse and watched the scramble proceed from confusion to chaos. He grinned broadly. Then he turned and calmly rode off, after ordering the men to collect the equipment, patch the harnesses, and repair the wreckage. Swearing and sweating, the battery repaired the damage. They had judged wrongly. It was the last attempt they were to make to confuse and confound their schoolteacherish, friendly but stern commanding officer. Within two weeks the battery was able to break loose four guns, ammunition carriages, wagons, field kitchens and huts, and be on the move in fourteen minutes, something of a record.

Captain Truman took over his command with prayer and a devout desire to do right and keep his hand on the throttle. For a month he kept the guardhouse well populated and exhausted all the profanity he knew and invented variations with the aptitude of an impresario. He learned that although his battery held a debonair agnosticism toward rank, they had real respect for a man who asked no quarter, expected no favors, and proved himself genuine and real. Truman slept in the mud with his battery, often without the protective shelter of a pup tent, while the rain streamed down into his face. He tramped in mud to his knees, and when the guns were stuck in the mire he put his shoulder to the wheel and grunted and strained along with his men. He granted leaves whenever possible and won many a dollar at poker and blackjack. When a Battery D man was given leave, Truman seldom failed to call him in and inquire after his finances. If he needed money, Truman would lend him 250 francs or more on his IOU.

Mixing a firm unyielding discipline with kindly favors to his men, and sharing with them the sweat and slime of the battlefield, Captain Truman created in his battery a loyalty and spirit that was unbeatable. The Kansas City Irishmen learned quickly to like and to respect him. Here was an officer who made them carry out the orders, who jailed them, who loaned them money, who drank cognac and vin rouge or vin blanc with them, but who never cringed before danger or remained idle while the others worked.

Lieutenant Colonel Edward V. Condon, a National Guard officer who served in Battery D, once said that "every man in that battery would have gone through Hell for Harry Truman. The night before the Meuse-Argonne offensive he gathered us around and made a little talk. It wasn't what you could call a speech, just a quiet talk like an older brother sometimes has with a younger boy. A few things that Harry Truman said that night still stick in my mind:

" 'I want to tell you this, too, fellows. Right tonight I'm where I want to be—in command of this battery. I'd rather be right here than be President of the United States. You boys are my kind. Now let's go in!' "

Generally before an offensive there had been such talks by Captain Truman, but this was the one which stayed in Colonel Condon's memory. The battery knew that it could carry out the Captain's orders for it had been fighting for months together during that final year of the war.

It had first gone into action on August 18, 1918, in the Vosges Mountains sector, a rather quiet place where the fighting consisted mostly of lobbing an occasional round of 75-millimeter shells some three miles over into the German lines. From August 18 to September 3 the battery remained in this salient. Then late one night orders came to move at once into the St. Mihiel sector. The big offensive then being

With hair closely cropped, First Lieutenant Truman is photographed in 1917. The next year, as a captain, he led his artillery battery through bitter fighting in France.

After World War I, Truman was promoted to major and continued his military training. Here, sporting a mustache, he takes part in Army maneuvers at Fort Riley, Kansas. Truman hates war but believes it often develops strong latent qualities of character.

mounted was almost at hand. All around, troops were being quietly entrained under cover of darkness for shipment to the new front; artillery batteries were disappearing overnight, and the mammoth Western Front war of maneuver was under way.

Since artillery was not mechanized in those days, Truman's Battery D consisted of four 75-millimeter guns with six horses for each gun, besides ammunition carts. Hurriedly, the battery began rooting up the spaded-in gun limbers, hitching up the teams, and within an hour were chugging off on one of the dinky French railroad trains. It was on this trip that Truman met Colonel Bennett Champ Clark, who was later to serve with him in the Senate of the United States.

At a small siding, the train stopped and Captain Truman walked into the little hut by the tracks. Clark was there with an armload of orders and maps. "Get off that train and get out of here," he shouted at Truman. "The enemy has been blasting this place: here are your orders and maps."

Truman took one look outside at a couple of dead horses by the train, and in twenty minutes his battery had the guns unshipped, the teams hitched, and was rattling off up the road while, behind, Bennett Clark laughed uproariously. It had been at least two days since a German shell had landed anywhere in the vicinity.

It was on September 6 in the Vosges Mountains that Truman and his battery fought what he was later to call "The Battle of Who Run." The battery was in position and Brigadier General Lucian G. Berry ordered a chlorine gas barrage. The order was for five hundred rounds pumped into a village position in the German lines, preceding an infantry bayonet attack. It was a dark night and the rain poured down in torrents. Truman's battery began lobbing the gas shells into the village. Suddenly a half-dozen German Howitzer shells crashed into and around the battery, killing six horses instantly.

"Run, boys! By God, they've got a bracket on us!" an unnamed sergeant screamed in panic as he took to his heels. The other men of Battery D bolted.

Standing in the midst of his battery, Truman yelled in a shout that rose above the crash of battle: "Hey!—Get back here! Help me hook up these horses and get this battery out of here!" There were more shells coming over, but the men took one look back at Truman, then returned and with shaking, hurried hands hooked in the traces and helped haul the battery back and to the right some three hundred yards to safety. The stubborn Kansas City Irish were not going to let this fellow with quiet courage outdo them.

The battery moved into position for the St. Mihiel offensive on the night of September 12, and at four o'clock in the morning it began firing. It was up close to the lines, and behind were the larger guns, still farther back the immense railway pieces that hurled gigantic shells into the enemy positions. The firing continued for an hour, and then at the zero hour near dawn, when the infantry went over the top, the battery elevated its sights and began firing on roads and villages farther behind the German line. For the next four days Captain Truman and his battery went unshaven and sleepless, with life a wearying, unbroken job of hitching up the guns, moving forward, unhitching, spading them in, firing several hundred rounds on machine gun nests or villages, hitching up and moving again.

Mile after mile of advance unwound itself, and the battery grew to hate the Kaiser, the German General Staff, and the enemy soldiers at every step and each pull of the lanyard.

This was the push that started the Germans reeling back to defeat. But they did not take it meekly. Their guns fired back. The wounded were coming back in streams, and dead littered the roadways of the advance. The batteries on either side of Battery D were badly shot up, but somehow, miraculously, Battery D escaped. On the night of September 16 the battery was pulled out of the St. Mihiel salient, loaded on another train and shipped into the Meuse-Argonne sector. It rested for a week, then moved up into position. It was on the night of September 25 that Truman delivered the homely talk that was to stay with Colonel Condon. The great offensive was ready for the jump-off.

The night was fairly calm. The enemy, nervous but not alerted to the impending offensive, threw over only a few shells. An occasional rifle crack sounded dimly. And then, past midnight, the guns began to open up. It started like a Missouri hailstorm on a tin roof; a gun at the left crashed through a round, then a salvo on the right, then two at once, a lull, then three, and finally a rising crescendo that became a roaring drumfire of flash and thunder.

Harry Truman stood directly behind his battery with a stop watch. The field maps were spread out on boxes of ammunition containing enough high explosive to kill off the entire battery if a shell came crashing in. The four guns opened up almost simultaneously. The artillerymen worked frantically, jamming shells home, yanking lanyards, tossing away the debris that seemed to pile up around each gun limber.

As his music teacher had done for him years before, Captain Truman counted off the time by his stop watch with metronomic regularity, for each gun to fire—"One—two—three—four. One—two—three—four." His voice, never strong, and always unaccustomed to extended use, grew ragged and hoarse. The barrels of the French 75's began to glow like fireflies in the early morning grayness, then changed to a coppery color before turning fiery red. Four cans of drinking water stood near by, and Truman ordered the men to toss their woolen blankets into the water, then drape them over the gun barrels. He pulled one gun from the battery, kept three firing with musical regularity and precision while the one was wrapped in the soaked blankets. Every ten minutes he pulled out another gun and substituted the one which had cooled off. That way each gun cooled ten minutes out of every thirty. It was necessary to speed up the three pieces' firing to keep up the rate that had been set for four, and each of the three active guns kept firing six shots per minute of high explosive.

The blankets smoked and burned, and new ones were tossed into the water and draped over the hot barrels. By eight o'clock that morning of September 26 Captain Truman's battery had fired three thousand rounds—a frenzied rate of cannonading. The bloody torrent of fire and steel ripped up the German front line trenches, hurling human bodies and broken bones over thousands of yards. Truman's explanation of the precision of his battery—which became something of a wonder in the 35th—was simple: "I was told where I had to fire and I had to fire there, or by God, it was my neck if I didn't."

All through that day, he played eloquently upon the four guns under his command. From Saturday morning until Tuesday night, his battery and himself fired, advanced, reset; fired, advanced, reset, and fired. In all of this time neither Truman nor his men had a wink of sleep. Men from other adjoining batteries wandered over to pick up the fine points of precision firing from Battery D—this muddy, unshaven crew that sweat and swore and worked like demons and seemed always to lay them right on the targets.

It was in this same offensive that Captain Truman nearly drew a court-martial trial on himself. One sunny afternoon as his battery was moving forward into a new position, he stood on a knoll with his binoculars and swept the hills and countryside ahead of him. He was drawing in his mind a pin-point map of the territory ahead, familiarizing himself

The Soldier

with the targets and the terrain. His glasses swung in a widening arc and suddenly he stiffened and grew still. There, some two thousand yards ahead and at one side, he saw clearly a German battery moving up into position to shell the advancing Americans. He ordered his battery to unhitch, spade in the timbers, and load. Then he calculated the distance, triangulated his fire, and gave the signal. The first two shots were overs, then two shorts. Captain Truman had what he wanted. He performed a fast calculation, reset the sights on the battery, and in less than two minutes laid down forty-one rounds in the middle of the German battery, scattering men and horses and guns over the hillside.

Ten minutes later his field telephone rang and he answered. A colonel farther back yelled, "What are you doing firing out of your sector? You know damned well where you are to fire. I'm going to have you court-martialed!"

"Go ahead!" Truman shouted back, summoning up some Kansas City oaths. "There was a German battery moving into position in plain sight of us. I'll never pass up a chance like that. We plastered 'em. Besides, I think it's a fool order anyway."

The colonel clicked the receiver. Truman's battery had fired over into a sector belonging to the 28th Division. He waited for days for the court-martial order which never arrived.

On October 3, the battery was pulled out of the Meuse-Argonne and sent to the Sommedieu-Verdun sector. It moved into position on October 16 and fought through this offensive to November 7, then was put in the second Meuse-Argonne offensive.

On the morning of November 11, at ten forty-five—fifteen minutes before the Armistice became official—Battery D fired its last salvo of high explosive shell on German positions near the little town of Hermaville, at 11,400 yards. It had fired six hundred rounds that day, and throughout the offensives it had fired some 14,000 rounds under Captain Truman's orders.

The batteries adjoining Truman's sustained 129 casualties and were badly shot up. Truman's battery had one killed and one wounded. At the final inspection of the 35th Division, General Pershing walked up to Captain Truman and asked how many men of the battery were lost in the fighting.

"One killed and one wounded, sir," Captain Truman said.

"I see," said Black Jack Pershing. "You weren't with the regiment all the time, were you?"

"Yes, sir, right in the middle of it, all through it!" Truman replied, and Pershing shook his head and passed on.

"I guess it was the praying those Kansas City Irish Catholics did," reminisces Truman the Baptist.

The battery gave Truman one excruciatingly painful and embarrassing moment. At Courcemont, the then Prince of Wales, Edward, informed General Pershing he would like to "inspect" the 35th. Pershing acquiesced and the men were ordered into formation. It was raining hard and they stood in mud and slush from 10 A.M. until 2 P.M. while the Prince inspected. Then he addressed the officers, while Battery D stood directly across a small creek. The little speech of praise and appreciation over, Truman leaped across the creek, sank in and slogged up out of the mud to march his battery away. Edward and General Pershing were standing less than twenty yards away when a Battery D man sang out: "Hey, Captain Truman! What did the little ——— —·— ——— say about freeing Ireland?"

If either the Prince or General Pershing heard the irreverent remark neither then disclosed it.

President Truman always explained his military career by saying, "I didn't do anything out of the ordinary. I was not wounded, and I got no citations of any kind." This is a little short of the truth. Officers who served with him described him—long before he became a United States senator —as one of the finest and toughest artillery officers in the whole army. He knew guns and he knew men. He knew the mud and numbing cold of rain and a bed on the ground, the gnaw of hunger when rations did not get up to the lines, and he was utterly unafraid. He was recommended for his Majority by Colonel Demm, his commanding officer of regimental canteen days, but before the promotion came through, he was discharged and promoted to a Major in the reserve corps.

He shipped back to the United States, landing in New York on May 6, 1919. His battery mates, as the boat pulled into New York harbor, presented Truman with a silver loving cup which they had secretly purchased, just to let the Captain know that any past grudges were forgiven.

Captain Harry went straight to the farm at Grandview, to keep a most important engagement.

Harry Truman considered, and still considers, himself a very lucky man when Bess Wallace said she would marry him. At thirty-five he was very excited after he had completed his bashful, somewhat embarrassed proposal at the Wallace home, and had received the answer he so much wanted to hear. Bess Wallace had had many chances to marry other men, but she had preferred to wait for the boy she had kept company with from those days in school together. She liked his sincerity, his truthfulness, and unassuming friendliness, and she had grown to love him through the years. Each had sort of understood even in high school eighteen years before that some day they would get married.

The ceremony was performed on June 28, 1919, in Trinity Episcopal Church at Independence. The church is one of the oldest in all the country around—a small, red brick structure with a basement that is used for meetings, church socials, and similar affairs. The day of the wedding, friends of the couple decorated the interior of the church with flowers taken in profusion from the gardens of their homes, and the chancel was banked with blossoms. The Reverend John W. Plunkett was severe in his dark attire, and Harry Truman was trembling in his gray suit, a color he even yet prefers.

The Soldier

Bess Wallace was a lovely bride. She wore a short, simply modeled white dress, a wide hat, and carried no flowers. Instead, as she walked to the altar accompanied by two cousins, Louise Wells and Helen Wallace, she held an Episcopal prayer book. It was a simple wedding, and friends crowded the little church to witness it. None in all the gathering were prouder than the boys of old Battery D who turned out almost to the last man, all in civilian clothes, to see Captain Harry married, with another buddy, Captain Theodore Marks, as best man.

When the ceremony was over, Harry and Bess Truman left the church, drove the Stafford car to the big old Gates-Wallace house at 219 North Delaware Street, and there received guests before they left for their honeymoon trip to Chicago and then to Detroit.

When they returned they moved into this roomy house which they have since acquired for themselves. Early in 1945 it looked quite worn and weatherbeaten, but since Truman became President it has had a fresh coat of white paint, and hereafter will serve as the summer White House, for the President intends to go back to Independence to visit.

It was in this same house that their daughter, Mary Margaret, was born on February 17, 1924. Bess Wallace preferred to have the baby at home, and the child was delivered by a stately, homely old gentleman who had long been the family physician, Dr. C. E. Krimminger, a doctor of recognized skill and learning in the town.

Shortly after Truman was married, he and his old Battery D buddies organized the Officers Reserve Corps No. 1 at Kansas City, and he never lost interest in military training and policy. For years thereafter he regularly took the summer "refresher" courses at Fort Leavenworth over in Kansas, across the Missouri River. Officers who served with him at these summer schools pronounced him one of the best.

When the United States went to war again on December 7, 1941, Truman went to the closet in his five-room apartment in Washington, D. C., pulled on the old olive drab pants and tunic. They fitted him. He was flat of stomach and lean through the shoulders, and weighed 170 pounds, only slightly heavier than on November 11, 1918.

He went immediately to General George C. Marshall, Chief of Staff, and offered his services. He said he wanted, if possible, to take command of an artillery battery.

General Marshall adjusted his glasses, said he appreciated it, but—

"Senator Truman, you've got a big job to do right up there at the Capitol, with your Investigating Committee. Besides, Senator, this is a young man's war. We don't need any old stiffs like you." The last remark was affectionately to the point. Truman was fifty-seven then.

But when General Marshall advised Truman that he was too old the Senator replied: "I am younger than you are, General Marshall."

"Yes," replied the General, three years Truman's senior,

"but I'm a general and you'd only be a colonel. You stay right where you are." This ended the discussion.

However, Truman complained to members of his Investigating Committee, and said, "Those were great days over in France with Battery D. What gets me is that I'm sitting around now and letting others do the fighting."

Throughout the years after the first World War, Truman kept in his home the heavy notebooks and service records he had kept as captain of Battery D. These records were vital in obtaining pension, medical and other benefits for his old war companions, and no one of them ever asked for help but what he got it. Annually, the men of Battery D held a reunion, the last one immediately after Truman's nomination as candidate for Vice-President.

Truman was a good soldier. And any member of Battery D would insist that Truman was an able officer and a tough one, deserving of almost any rank.

From the time he took command, after five other officers had been broken out, no one in Battery D had ever doubted who issued the orders, nor did any man deny that here, in this unassuming officer, was a man of courage. He did not attempt the foolhardy, but he never ran or cringed in the face of danger.

In the lulls between fighting he would take a bayonet or stick and draw battle diagrams in the mud of France and lecture his men on the great military engagements of history.

Truman could recall from memory the plans and execution of Civil War battles, the mistakes that were made, and the tactics that failed. He knew intimately the lives of Robert E. Lee and Stonewall Jackson, the only two generals whose pictures were to hang later in his Senate office. He could recite details of the fighting at Thermopylae and Tours and had studied the Napoleonic wars down to the minutest maneuver.

Harry Truman learned war the way he has learned almost everything else in his life—the hard way, as a frontline soldier enduring the hardships, seeing the misery and accepting the dangers.

Chapter Five

Politician

THE YEAR HE RETURNED FROM FRANCE, HARRY Truman decided to go into business, leaving brother Vivian to run the Grandview farm. This decision turned out to be heartbreaking and costly—one that kept his nose to the grindstone for years.

Eddie Jacobson visited him and they talked over the days when they ran the regimental canteen at Fort Sill, how they had in six months piled up a $15,000 profit on a $2,200 investment. It was now 1919 and the war was over. Prices were good. Eddie knew merchandise. Truman had a little money saved up. It looked as if business would be good for years.

"Why don't we go in together, Harry?" Eddie asked. "We made money in the canteen and we can make it in Kansas City. We ought to have a clothing store, and I know one that can be bought. It's right close to the Muelbach Hotel."

The pair talked over prospective profits, and the job of raising money—an initial investment of about $20,000—to get started. They decided to become clothing merchants. They set up store at 104 West 12th Street, across from the

Muelbach, with Eddie acting as buyer and markup man, Truman hopping counters, selling neckties, shirts, belts, socks, and suits. The store was a going concern. The first year the firm of Truman & Jacobson sold $100,000 of merchandise and showed a tidy return on its investment.

Clothing, however, is one of the most precarious of all merchandising ventures. A grocery store is calculated to turn over its entire stock every thirty days in the aggregate—that is, sell out and reorder entirely. People have to have groceries whether times are good or bad, for eating does not stop. A clothing stock, on the other hand, expertly managed, will not be turned over more than once every three or four months. The temptation to say "charge it" when ordering a suit is greater than when purchasing a pound of bacon. And when hard times come, men wear their suits longer, thinner, and buy them cheaper.

This is exactly what happened to Truman & Jacobson. The second year business slumped. Bills got harder to pay. The credit accounts of the store were getting too large, and attempts to collect in money were becoming less and less fruitful.

In 1922, the firm failed. The depression of 1921—decline of farm prices, wages, and the first foreshadowings of the apple peddlers and soup lines of 1930-31—caused the store to go under. The crash made little noise in Kansas City, but it was a major tragedy to Harry Truman. He borrowed what he could from banks on the security of the family farm, and began paying off.

Politician

This process of repayment continued thereafter for almost fifteen years. In the end, Truman repaid every dime that he owed—more than $20,000. Some adjustments of debt were made, scaled down, but the repayment was complete on the final establishment of money owed.

Truman repaid thousands of dollars out of his subsequent salaries, and for years the family lived a frugal, almost parsimonious existence.

Just as he had learned soldiering, learned farming, and learned to play the piano, Harry Truman was learning the rudiments of business and finance. This load of debt and problem of repayment instilled in the Truman family a deep and fervent knowledge of the value of a dollar and, sometimes, its inaccessibility. The family had always been careful buyers. Now they became very careful. They learned to know values and to seek them out. They discovered how to save a dollar instead of squandering it. Their pleasures were simple and few: an occasional movie, sometimes a concert, a drive out into the rolling green hills around Independence.

At Camp Doniphan, a young lieutenant named Jim Pendergast had served with Captain Truman and admired him. Back in Kansas City his uncle Tom Pendergast was boss of one of the most powerful political machines in all the broad expanse of the United States. Uncle Tom controlled Kansas City and a balance of power in the state of Missouri. He was a big, heavy man, pure Irish with an Irishman's flair for hard-boiled, practical politics. Heavy pouches

The stately Truman residence in Independence, Missouri, which now serves as the Summer White House. It was built in the 1860's by the First Lady's grandfather, a successful flour miller. When Truman was courting his wife, he often drove up in front in his four-cylinder, 1913-model Stafford automobile.

Harry Truman (in foreground) leaning against the counter of his haberdashery store, which he ran with Eddie Jacobson, in Kansas City. In the rear stand several cronies of war days who used to come in to buy a shirt or swap the latest gossip. The firm of Truman & Jacobson failed in 1922, and it took Truman fifteen years to pay off his debts.

sagged under his eyes. He had a willingness to help those who voted right—meaning with Pendergast—and a predilection for squelching those who didn't. Uncle Tom had many and varied interests in contracting companies and cement firms, and it was common knowledge in Missouri's Democratic administrations that contractors awarded road construction jobs were expected to buy Uncle Tom's cement at premium prices.

Pendergast's second-floor office at 1908 Main Street was modest and unpretentious, but its roster of callers—governors, senators, state legislators, congressmen, ward heelers—all testified that it was a fountain of influence. Here in the construction company, politics was a major industry and building only incidental.

In 1922 at about the time Truman and Jacobson were pulling down the haberdashery sign and turning the keys over to their creditors, a harried group of political chiefs was hunting a strong candidate for the eastern district county judge of Jackson County. This group included Jim Pendergast, who acted as a sort of front-line lieutenant for Uncle Tom and the "goat" faction of Democratic politicians. The "goat" faction was the Pendergast group, and their opponents within the party comprised the "rabbits," a faction ruled by the late Congressman Joseph (Uncle Joe) Shannon. The two groups were at open war in every primary, and then, the battle over, seldom failed to consolidate their forces to lick the Republicans.

Politician

The perennial fights between the "goats" and the "rabbits" not only agitated Kansas City but kept rural Jackson County in political turmoil. Soon after the Truman family moved to Independence, Father John Truman had become a close personal friend of James M. Callahan, one of eastern Jackson County's leading lawyers and head of the "goat" faction in the Independence area. John Truman had aligned himself with Callahan and young Harry Truman was practically weaned on "goat" politics.

Also, Harry Truman had formed a warm friendship with young Jim Pendergast and with his father Mike Pendergast, an older brother of Boss Tom, who used to visit his son at Camp Doniphan. Mike controlled the tenth political ward in Kansas City while Boss Tom ruled the first ward.

In talks with his father, young Jim Pendergast suggested that a soldier should be the candidate for the eastern district county judgeship. He advised that no better man could be found than Captain Truman, former commander of Battery D, since many ex-Battery D members lived right in the teeming tenth ward. Mike Pendergast fell in with this proposal and spoke to Truman about it. But he received no definitive answer. Truman was not particularly interested just then.

The "goats" thereupon went to a gray-haired man named William Southern, a Democrat and editor of the *Independence Examiner*, a daily newspaper with the greatest Jackson County circulation outside of the *Kansas City Star*. Bill

Politician

Southern wrote a weekly Bible column which was widely syndicated. He had met Harry Truman many times at church and Sunday-school meetings. He told the "goats" they should insist that Truman run for judge and he talked personally to Truman in such terms. Truman thought it over again and finally told Southern that if there were no strings attached to the support of the "goat" faction, he would make the race. He came to the decision because he had always been interested in politics, and besides, the clothing store was gone and he needed work.

This was the beginning of as strange a political coalition as has been seen almost anywhere. Ultimately, Tom Pendergast was to land in the penitentiary and Harry Truman was to go to the White House.

The Pendergast machine was ruled by a hand of iron. Uncle Tom was no parlor politician, and he knew all the tricks of nasty infighting. His methods in a campaign were ridiculously simple: gather up all the money possible, spend it freely where needed, pick your own man, and drive the machine along behind him. If necessary, get some stooges in the primary to split the vote of any candidate threatening to upset the machine politician, and never hesitate to do political favors or demand support in return.

Uncle Tom decided to run Truman for the county judgeship, and Truman was confident for, as he said later, "I had kinfolks in every precinct." They would go out and beat the drums for him. The "rabbits" put up E. E. Montgomery, a banker at Blue Springs, and two independents entered the race, George Shaw, a road contractor, and James Compton, a judge serving by appointment. Truman had an old Dodge roadster, its fenders battered and its motor wheezing and puffing at every slight grade. He bumped and rattled over the county in this machine, and when the votes were counted he had won by a plurality of five hundred ballots. He served out his first term with credit, then ran again but was defeated. He was also studying law at nights at the Kansas City School of Law, no outstanding college but a sound one, and he liked the law. His instructor, Arnwell L. Cooper, recalls that Truman was a first-rate student and one of the leaders in his law class. In spare times Truman took lessons and learned to swim at the Kansas City Athletic Club.

It must have been a strange first meeting between Tom Pendergast and Harry Truman. Truman asked for Pendergast's support and in the same breath told the political boss that while he was a loyal Democrat he expected, if elected, to be and remain scrupulously honest, to work hard and by a record of honesty and fair dealing to make whatever votes he could for the Pendergast Democrats.

After his defeat in 1924 at the end of his first term in the county court, Truman looked around for another job. He helped organize the Kansas City Automobile Club and soon had a successful venture going with some hundreds of members. The club supplied road information, maps, and a variety of services, besides working in the interest of more and better roads in Missouri. Within less than two years,

Truman had ballooned the membership to more than three thousand. But he yearned for a political comeback.

In Missouri the county judges need not be lawyers. They try no cases and hear no suits. They are elected for two years as "judges" who run the county's business. They let contracts, draw up the budgets, allocate monies to institutions and civic developments, recommend tax schedules for public referendum, plan public works, manage the county charitable institutions and grant pensions to the poor. The hand of Pendergast was shoulder deep in all of these doings, for Pendergast not only ran Kansas City; he manipulated the state.

In 1926 Truman wanted to run for County Collector of Jackson County, a position that paid up to $25,000 a year in fees, but Tom Pendergast demurred, saying the job had been promised to a lifelong "goat" Democrat. Instead, Pendergast offered Truman the nomination for presiding judge of the county court. He reluctantly accepted Boss Tom's offer, although in so doing he offended Mike Pendergast, who wanted Truman to file for County Collector regardless of any prior agreement. Truman ran for presiding judge and was elected by a margin of 16,000 votes. Because both the "goats" and "rabbits" had been beaten in the bitter election of 1924, they had consolidated forces and were agreed on the ticket without a fight. The county then was paying banks 6 per cent on the revenue anticipation notes it sold to finance its government, and it could under the law sell only 90 per cent of the amount it fairly expected to receive from its taxes. Truman went to the Kansas City banks and asked for a reduction in the interest rates, and then went back and told the court that the banks had talked as if they thought he was trying to steal from them by such a proposition. He boarded a train for Chicago, talked to the bankers there, and succeeded in getting the interest cut to $4\frac{1}{2}$ per cent by marketing the notes in Chicago. By the time he left the county court, he had helped to bring the interest rates down to $1\frac{1}{2}$ per cent.

In 1928 Truman ran again for presiding judge, and the big issue in this campaign was honesty—would the Pendergast outfit be allowed to steal Jackson County blind?

The year before, Truman had surveyed the county and proposed a road-construction program, requiring a ten-million-dollar bond outlay. Truman had also suggested a new county court house for Kansas City and renovation for the one in Independence.

At the same time, Kansas City was also planning improvements, including many new public buildings in the Kansas City area. With the help of a committee of one hundred, they expected to put over a 32-million-dollar bond issue.

Truman went to both Pendergast and Shannon and told them he thought Jackson County should participate in the building plan, or, at least, in the road-improvement program. Pendergast did not think that the county's $11,500,000 share of the bond issue would carry; such a proposition never had. But Truman insisted it would because "I intend to tell the taxpayers exactly what I'm going to do and I will do it."

Boss Tom laughed and said, "Tell them what you please."

"I will," said Truman, "and then I will carry it out."

"Well," replied Pendergast, "if you carry the bond issue you can certainly carry it out." Shannon and Pendergast controlled the majority on the county court, and Truman needed this assurance.

But to the voters the real question was: Would Pendergast contractors or Pendergast cement build those roads at fancy prices? If that question could be resolved in the negative, the bonds would carry and the improvements would be made. Newspapers were asking whether the fund was, in fact, for public improvement, or a silver lining for the pockets of the Pendergast organization.

Truman went out and met the issue head-on. He told the voters:

"The bond issue is going to carry. If you elect me, I pledge you that every cent of contracts for roads will be let to the lowest bidder in open bidding." Truman repeated this in scores of speeches throughout the county. He won, the bond issue carried, and Jackson County sat back to watch.

The surveys were made, and the county court advertised for bids. Immediately all the jackals that clung to or made up the Pendergast machine swarmed into Harry Truman's office. They urged him to dole out the contracts, not to ask for bids, not to shop around for the low bidders. They would build the roads, they said, and do a good job, a money-saving job; why spend a lot of money advertising in the Republican *Kansas City Star* that every day was editorially calling Truman and Pendergast a pair of thieves?

"I promised the people these roads would be built under contracts assigned to the low bidders in wide-open bidding," Truman said. "The roads will be built that way. There's no use asking anything else."

Within a few days Tom Pendergast telephoned. He would like to see the Presiding Judge. Truman left the county courthouse and went to Pendergast's office. There he found the same group of contractors who had insisted that he conveniently forget all about his campaign pledges. Pendergast repeated their arguments and asked why they couldn't be given contracts.

He did not ask it as a demand or a command but seemingly as a matter of information. Truman's reply was immediate: "Because I pledged the people that contracts would be let to the low bidders on open bidding. That's the way it will be done."

Tom Pendergast hunched around to the contractors and growled, "Well, see there, I told you he wouldn't change. He says they'll be let on low bids. That's the way they'll be let. Now get out of my office and leave me alone."

When the contractors had left the office, Pendergast said to Truman, "You carry out the contract with the taxpayers just as you told them you would carry it out, and I will support you." Truman did, and the money was spent as it should have been. Later, Truman obtained an additional $3,500,000 for his building program and this, too, was carried out on exactly the same basis.

"Tom Pendergast never asked me to do a dishonest deed," Harry Truman said not once but many times. "He knew I wouldn't do it if he asked it. He was always my friend. He was always honest with me, and when he made a promise he kept it. If he told me something, I knew it was the truth. When Tom Pendergast was down and out, a convicted felon, the Kansas City and St. Louis papers demanded that I denounce him. I refused and then they denounced me.

"I wouldn't kick a friend and I wouldn't kick him when he was down. The newspapers poured it on me, but in public office you can't let the newspapers dictate your life and thought."

It was not that Harry Truman condoned Pendergast's thefts and his evasions of Federal income taxes, but rather that Tom Pendergast had befriended him, had been personally honest with him, and he was not going to renounce a friend. That was the way Truman saw it morally.

The roads were built in Jackson County, and when the Federal Bureau of Investigation and the Treasury income tax division descended on Tom Pendergast they moved in also on Harry Truman. They combed the files and amassed an amazing record of graft and thievery against Pendergast but found not one iota of corruption in all of Truman's career. When in 1944 Truman was nominated for Vice-President the man who prosecuted and sent Pendergast to prison, District Attorney Maurice Milligan at Kansas City, was asked by a reporter about Truman's record. Milligan said, yes, he had examined Truman's record but had found nothing of dishonesty and nothing deserving censure.

Two of the men associated with Truman on the Jackson County court have publicly upheld his administration as clean, honest and honorable. They were N. T. Veatch, a Republican of Kansas City, and Major General E. M. Stayton, retired, a Democrat and once commander of the 35th Missouri National Guard Division.

"I never heard of any undue waste or corruption during his administration," stated General Stayton. "He administered the . . . program with the highest degree of efficiency, economy and integrity." Veatch's report was equally forthright and complimentary.

There is no doubt that had Harry Truman been vulnerable to charges of corruption or graft or theft, the Federal Government would have prosecuted him. Milligan and the Milligan family were political enemies of Truman. District Attorney Milligan literally mowed down the Pendergast organization, but Harry Truman's bill of health was clean and his record unimpeachable.

Truman had hardly entered into politics when his opponents spread the report that he had belonged to the Ku Klux Klan. The issue was raised in his second campaign for

Politician

county judge, and he met it squarely, demanded proof and got none. He then demonstrated that instead of belonging to the Klan he had denounced it fervently throughout Jackson County.

During the 1944 Vice-Presidential campaign, hostile newspapers, barely before the election, published a purported affidavit to the effect that Truman had indeed belonged to this nefarious organization. The charge was as false as if he had been accused of being in the secret pay of Adolf Hitler. As a matter of fact Truman himself was a high Mason and, furthermore, two of his close advisers on the campaign train were Catholics, Matthew J. Connelly and Edward McKim. The public, recognizing yellow journalism, disregarded the accusation.

The charges that Truman had once belonged to the Ku Klux Klan were made late in October, calculated to have the most effect upon the election and offering the least opportunity for rebuttal before the voting on November 7.

The Klan charges made during the Vice-Presidential campaign were based on such flimsy evidence and were so patently unfair, that their effect on the election was nil. For a while Truman debated with himself whether to file suits for libel to expose in all its nakedness the injustice of the publications. He finally abandoned the notion after discussing the whole affair with his wife, Bess. They concluded that should he take the matter to court, he would only prolong the memory of an unsavory falsity that the public was quickly forgetting.

Politician

The affair was a cruel and calculated attack on a man who holds dear, above all other things, his honesty and his integrity.

Truman is proud that he is a politician, and he has never been known to offer any excuses for the profession. He considers it honorable and decent, and readily admits that he plays politics. "A politician is the ablest man in government, and when he's dead they call him a statesman," he reasons.

He accepted Pendergast support for the simple reason that in Missouri in the 1920's it was practically hopeless to run for office—in Jackson County or the statewide races—without machine help.

In many ways Harry Truman was a valuable asset to the Pendergast organization. He regularly ran from 30,000 to 50,000 votes ahead of the machine slate, and picked up votes for the machine. It, in return, supplied him with tens of thousands of votes which could be counted as certain even before the polls opened.

Then, too, Harry Truman supplied an element and façade of honesty and integrity which Pendergast could hardly claim without him. His terms as county judge had been marked by a bi-partisan responsibility on the county court, and by an absence of graft in this branch of the government. Schools, care of the insane, the roads—all had shown a marked improvement. And the Pendergast organization could, with no small pride, point to this efficient, likeable fellow and his honest administration when charges of corruption, theft, political favoritism and governmental chicanery were raised.

Truman was one Pendergast man who went to the highest office, freely admitting that politics was his profession, and arrived there clean and happy though by financial standards relatively poor.

Chapter Six

Senator

HARRY TRUMAN HAS SAID MANY TIMES THAT HE never really wanted to be anything other than Senator from Missouri.

On April 10, 1945, Vice-President Truman stood in front of the white marble dais in the Senate chamber talking with a group of reporters he knew and admired for their fairness and industry.

"Boys," he said slowly, "here's the only place for me, right here in the Senate. But I feel frustrated in the Vice-Presidency. All I've ever wanted to be is Senator. Maybe some day I'll get to come back as a Senator."

Less than forty-eight hours later he was President of the United States.

Two weeks before, while presiding over the Senate, he had spied former Senator Prentiss M. Brown of Michigan listening to the debate at the back of the chamber. Truman summoned a page boy and scrawled a little penciled note:

Dear Prentiss, he wrote, *Ain't it hell. We're both muzzled now. You have my sympathy. Harry.*

When Truman began his first term in the Senate in 1935,

he was aware and sensitive of the stigma that others had spread like a mantle over his election and his character.

Here was an obscure county judge whom boss-ruled machine politics had raised to the eminence of United States Senator, though such had happened many times before in American politics. Harry Truman knew the hard, political facts of life. He sought a political career. He wanted to be an office holder, not an also-ran. It was simple arithmetic to figure that to be elected he needed the support of those who had the votes on election day. When the cry of bossism was again raised during Truman's campaign for Vice-President, he observed realistically "a boss-ruled political machine is a bad thing, if the machine is not on your side."

Yet when Harry Truman was sworn in as Senator, he sensed that his background was unpromising and his future uncertain. Some of the more venerable statesmen in the Senate gave him a wide berth. His Democratic colleague, Bennett Champ Clark, was not even on friendly political terms with him.

Truman realized that his arrival in the Senate had been, in a sense, a political accident. When in 1926 he had asked Boss Pendergast to support him for county collector, he had visions of serving in the job for a few years until he could pay off his debts on the salary and fees it afforded, and then retire to the farm to spend the rest of his days there. It was fortunate that Tom Pendergast had promised the job to another. Truman had carried on manfully as county judge, instituted a building and budget reform program that with

Pendergast support had won re-election by a 58,000 vote margin in 1930.

It was at this time that Truman began to look to Washington, and to think of running for Congress. In 1932, because it had failed to redistrict under the 1930 census, Missouri elected all of its Congressmen at large. In 1933 the legislature met and did redistrict the state. Harry Truman was in the thick of that session at Jefferson City, and when the redistricting law was signed he had just what he wanted —the Fourth Missouri District comprised of rural Jackson County, an area where he felt he was sure of overwhelming support and steady re-election. In 1934 he wanted to run for Congress, but again Boss Tom said no. He had promised that district to C. Jasper Bell.

Politics were hot in Missouri that year. In 1932, both the "goats" and "rabbits" of Pendergast and Shannon had fought vainly against the nomination of Bennett Champ Clark of St. Louis, and both had taken a sound drubbing. The old sores of that fight still festered in the party. There was talk that despite President Roosevelt's popularity, the state might re-elect its Republican Senator Roscoe Patterson.

The state was conducting a referendum on a road bond issue and Harry Truman, at the suggestion of state officials, had taken the stump to support it. He had spoken in some thirty-five counties, and gradually the ambition to run for governor had begun to dawn upon him.

There is a story that is purely erroneous that Truman in that year went to Boss Tom and again asked his support

Wide World

As Presiding Judge of the Jackson County Court in Missouri, Truman still wears his Army discharge button in his coat lapel.

Truman and his mother in 1934, following his election to the United States Senate. Old Mrs. Truman is not overwhelmed by her son's rise to world prominence. When she visited Washington after he became President, she admonished crowds of reporters and bystanders at the airport by commenting, "Oh, fiddlesticks!"

for collector of revenue, and was told, "You can't have it, Harry. I've already promised it to another. The best I can do for you is United States Senator." And there is another embellishment that later Boss Tom said he had supported Truman to show Missouri that "I could send an office boy to the United States Senate." There is no truth to either version.

In May of that same year, 1934, while Truman was speaking in south central Missouri for the bond issue at Warsaw, he received a call from Sedalia. It was James P. Aylward, the Democratic State Chairman, and with him was nephew Jim Pendergast. They wanted Truman to meet them at the Bothwell Hotel in Sedalia. Truman drove over to see them, and they urged him to run for the Senate, promising Boss Tom's support. Truman said he wanted to run for governor, but they made it clear he couldn't get support for that office. So Harry Truman ran for the Senate.

Whether Pendergast expected Truman to win is not and never will be known. Certainly when Truman announced his candidacy, the voters of Missouri greeted the news with apathy. Like most primary elections in America, the average citizen did not know what was going on at the ward clubs and cared less. This was politics—a game for the professionals who understood the rules and had the stomach to fight for the spoils.

The leading Democratic candidate at the time was a popular ex-Congressman, Jacob Milligan, brother of the attorney who was later to convict Pendergast, who had the eastern Missouri support of Bennett Champ Clark and his strong machine in St. Louis.

It was the Pendergast machine against the St. Louis machine, with the outcome to be settled by rural Missouri voters, those political agnostics who do not hesitate to vote one way in óne election and diametrically contrariwise in the next. The Clark-Milligan machine blanketed the state with speeches denouncing bossism. Truman was depicted as an errand boy for Boss Tom, and Tom Pendergast as having his hand deep in the pockets of Missouri and now reaching out to tap the Federal Treasury. The Pendergast machine replied with assertions that Milligan was a Bennett Clark stooge, that Clark wanted to be two Senators instead of one, and that he had delusions of becoming President. It was a bitter, mud-slinging battle with Truman, in the earlier stages, distinctly the underdog.

Bennett Clark, a master of scathing oratory and with a flair for finding and portraying the ridiculous in any situation, stumped for Milligan. However, at a crucial moment, Congressman John J. Cochran of St. Louis, a red-haired, dynamic man with a solid Democratic record, entered the primary contest. He fought both Truman and Milligan. There was talk that Cochran was injected by Pendergast to split the Milligan vote in St. Louis. Whether this was true or not, that was the net result of Cochran's participation. Truman was nominated by a plurality of 40,000 votes and was elected in the fall, displacing the incumbent Republican Senator Patterson.

Senator

It was this background that caused a cloud to hang over Harry Truman when he took his Senate seat, and he was fully aware of it as he often confessed later. In his first speeches in the Senate he claimed no other distinction than that he was just "a farm boy from Jackson County."

The first four years in the Senate were plodding years. Truman struggled vigorously to plow a straight furrow, as he had done on the farm. He lived quietly, remained silent, and worked hard. He studied voluminous reports of committee hearings. He read faithfully the *Congressional Record* and the newspapers, and spent long hours in the reading room of the Library of Congress. He observed the men with whom he worked and who shared the responsibilities of the Senate. One of the first to accept him was Carl Hatch of New Mexico; another was John Nance Garner, the Vice-President. A third was Burton K. Wheeler of Montana, for Truman was placed on his Interstate Commerce Committee. Wheeler soon realized that Truman was a sincere man and a diligent worker—if anything, overly sensitive of his own limitations.

Meanwhile Truman's retentive mind continued to sweep up and catalogue every scrap of personal and political information about each of his colleagues. He knew which men were conservative and which liberal, and understood the motives and reasons for their views. He soon found out which men worked hard and which ones loafed. He listened to the political worries and troubles of each one. He knew the personal and political prejudices of the Senators; even their favorite food and drink, the books they liked to read, their stories, their secret ambitions, the strengths and weaknesses of every member.

Truman never missed an opportunity to render, if possible and justified, some favor to another Senator. He was friendly, considerate, and helpful by nature. As time went by Truman's relations warmed with Bennett Champ Clark, son of the Speaker who, in the 1912 Baltimore Convention, had barely lost the nomination to Woodrow Wilson. But the pair handled Missouri's end of national politics in an atmosphere of armistice rather than friendliness.

These were the apprentice years for Harry Truman. His first promotion came from Senator Wheeler. An investigation of the railroad system was voted, and the inquiry was delegated to the Interstate Commerce Committee which Wheeler headed. Wheeler hired a brilliant attorney, Max Lowenthal, and then turned the entire investigation over to Harry Truman who was made chairman of the subcommittee.

Truman's knowledge of railroads was largely confined to riding the Missouri Pacific and the Baltimore and Ohio from Kansas City to Washington and to his youthful, boisterous days as timekeeper on the Santa Fe. He set out at once to remedy this deficiency. For months thereafter, while Wheeler was mending political fences in Montana, Senator Truman conducted the railroad investigation with fairness and extreme thoroughness. Railroad attorneys had no occasion to complain that they were being mishandled by the committee. The Chairman was always ready and eager to accept evidence on both sides. He went to the bottom of things, and it was clear from the record and from his conduct that he sought only the truth as he saw it. The result was the enactment of a national transportation act which Truman largely wrote, with Lowenthal's and Wheeler's assistance. Later, Truman also wrote most of the Civil Aeronautics Act.

The railroad inquiry was the first real opportunity Truman had to establish himself as a Senator of importance and caliber. His performance earned the respect of his colleagues, and gradually those who had regarded him with cool reserve began to thaw out toward the mild-mannered, sincere man from Missouri.

Predominantly, Senator Truman voted with the administration, although he did desert the fold to vote against a $4,800,000,000 relief appropriation. And in 1936 when Joseph T. Robinson of Arkansas died and the great struggle for leadership of the Senate ensued with Roosevelt backing Alben W. Barkley of Kentucky against the conservatives' Pat Harrison of Mississippi, Truman's vote was in doubt. A call went from Democratic Chairman Jim Farley's office in Washington to Boss Pendergast in Colorado Springs, asking him to "line up Harry on the right side." Pendergast telephoned Truman, and asked him to vote for Barkley.

"Look here, Harry," he said, "Jim Farley just called and asked me if I couldn't talk to you about voting for Barkley. Can't you do that?"

"No, Tom, I can't," Truman answered. "I've made up my mind to vote for Pat Harrison of Mississippi and I'm going to do it."

"Well, Harry," old Tom said, "I told him you were the contrariest guy in the world, so I guess that's that."

Truman voted for Pat Harrison, but Barkley became Majority Leader.

On the Appropriations Committee, Truman worked long, tedious hours and sought to acquaint himself thoroughly with the mass of wearying and dreary detail that passed across the committee tables or was lodged in the reams of testimony taken in executive sessions. He was particularly interested in military appropriations and served on this sub-committee. His philosophy was to give the Army what it needed and to require a strict accounting. His knowledge of military expenditures and military procedure, thus gained, was to be invaluable later when he set out to investigate the gigantic 250 billion dollar national defense and war program. A man with lesser knowledge and experience would have been lost in its maze of staggering expenses.

In the 1940 Senatorial election Truman had the closest call of his political career. A crusading Federal District Attorney at Kansas City, Maurice Milligan, brother of Jacob Milligan whom Truman had defeated in the previous election, resigned to run against Truman for the Democratic nomination. Milligan had been prosecuting with zeal, sending Pendergast politicians to jail. Two hundred and seventy-eight of Pendergast's ward heelers and election officers in

Kansas City were ultimately indicted for ballot frauds, and Milligan sent 258 of them to the penitentiary. He had even succeeded the year before in convicting Boss Tom himself.

Pendergast in his prosperous days had lived grandly. He had, said many a Missourian and many a newspaper, stolen the state blind over a period of years. He had wagered as much as two million dollars on the race tracks in a single year, and had lost as much as six hundred thousand dollars. However, his actual financial status was not revealed until 1945 when his will was filed after his death. Then Kansas City residents learned the almost unbelievable facts. The safety deposit box in which some had averred might be found half the wealth of Missouri yielded only two one-thousand-dollar government bonds; cash and bank deposits amounting to less than five thousand dollars. His entire personal estate, after deducting a debt of $107,609.84, amounted to only $13,615.38.

It was his gambling losses which eventually brought him to prison. Milligan's investigators discovered that in 1935 and 1936 Boss Tom had not reported for income tax $460,-000. He had taken this as part payment on a $750,000 bribe he was to receive in return for "fixing" for a group of fire insurance companies a dispute with the state of Missouri over some ten million dollars due policyholders as rebates on excessive charges. It was by means of this bribe that he sought to recover from his gambling losses.

Milligan had sent Boss Tom to Leavenworth Penitentiary for fifteen months for tax evasion, and had him under a five-year probationary sentence on another count. Otto Higgins, the Kansas City director of police, had also gone to prison and so had Emmett O'Malley, the Pendergast state commissioner of insurance, and Matt Murray, the Pendergast state director of the Works Progress Administration. The Pendergast machine was beginning to show unmistakable signs of disintegration.

Milligan was a state figure in Missouri, and his campaign was pitched on one theme: get rid of the Pendergast stooge, Harry Truman!

Missouri's considerably popular Governor Lloyd C. Stark of Hannibal, in northeast Missouri, likewise entered the race. He was counting on the farm vote, and reasoned that Milligan and Truman each would finish off the other. It was, indeed, a retrogressive farmer who had not at one time or another planted in his orchard some of the Governor's famous "Stark's Delicious" apple trees, ordered from the Hannibal nursery. The name of Stark was a farm byword in Missouri. Then, too, there had been talk that Stark might be appointed Secretary of the Navy by President Roosevelt. And at the Chicago convention Stark had been a receptive, if unsuccessful, candidate for the nomination for Vice-President—until Roosevelt named Henry Wallace as his running mate.

Governor Stark had supported Harry Truman in 1934, and when he ran for governor in 1936 Stark sought the aid and assistance of the Pendergast organization. At that time he did not know how to approach Boss Tom, but he was on friendly terms with Truman, calling often at his office in Washington, and was only slightly less friendly with Senator Clark. At Stark's request, the two Senators went to New York and met Boss Tom in his suite at the Waldorf-Astoria soon after he had disembarked from an Italian luxury liner following a tour of Europe. They told Pendergast what was in Stark's mind, that he wanted Pendergast's support, and Truman warmly urged that Stark was a dependable, loyal Democrat. At the time there were reports that Senator Clark was less enthusiastic, but the two Senators carried back word to Stark that if he could round up the support of county Democratic leaders in a sizable portion of rural Missouri, Pendergast would support him, and they told him the men to see. Stark had followed instructions. Pendergast had kept his pledge, and the nurseryman was elected governor of Missouri in 1936.

It was a bitter fight in Missouri during the 1940 election. There was little doubt that the Roosevelt administration wanted Milligan to win.

In 1938, Senator Clark had obtained Milligan's appointment as Federal Attorney and Truman had aggressively fought the nomination in the Senate. President Roosevelt disregarded his protests, and newspapers in and out of Missouri cried loudly that Truman's opposition was a "dirty job" he was ordered to perform by Boss Pendergast. On February 15, 1938, Truman took the floor to protest against the nomination and asked the Senate to reject Milligan. Red-faced and confident, Bennett Champ Clark sat by with a pocket full of notes, the outline of a bitter and critical speech. He did not deliver it. He waited until Truman had finished; then called for a vote.

By a voice vote the Senate confirmed Milligan, and only Truman voted in the negative.

Yet it was in the same year, 1938, that Clark was losing political ground in Missouri and needed the support of the Pendergast organization. And it was Harry Truman who wanted him to have it. In Maryville, Missouri, early in April, Truman made a speech endorsing Clark and was booed by an audience in his home state for the first and only time. Then he made another speech for Clark in Springfield a few days later. By these endorsements he forced Pendergast to support Clark.

By the time the election year 1940 came around, Pendergast was in prison and Clark chose neither to support nor attack his personal choice, Maurice Milligan, the District Attorney. He backed Truman, though he made no speeches in his behalf and did not declare publicly for Truman's candidacy until a few days before the primary election. He confined his campaigning to issuing press statements against Governor Stark, who had waged unceasing war on Pendergast after having been elected with his support four years before. Clark referred to Stark's "ill-fated, short-lived, and ludicrous candidacy for Vice-President at Chicago," and ridiculed reports that Stark would be named Secretary of the Navy, Secretary of War, Postmaster General, or for any other Federal position of dimension and stature.

Senator

The newspapers of the state were almost unanimously against Truman, and the *Kansas City Star* and *Times*, scenting a political kill, raised a great hue and cry against bossism which the press of the state took up. The powerful *St. Louis Post-Dispatch* ran one of its classic Fitzpatrick cartoons just before the August primary date, showing two mammoth trucks, one labeled Stark and the other Milligan, in a headlong crash with Truman depicted as driving a little kiddycar between. It was labeled "No place for a kiddycar."

Political wiseacres counted Truman out far in advance of the primary, and Truman himself was not optimistic of his chances. He was to say later that this was the bitterest, dirtiest political fight he had ever witnessed. There were few charges or insinuations that were not used, and "thief" was a parlor word during the campaign. The night of the primary, Truman went to bed about midnight, a disillusioned and sorely tried man. He was 11,000 votes behind Milligan and apparently defeated. When he got up in the morning the late returns showed that he was renominated by a slim 8,400 vote margin. The state had been shaken to its heels by the bitter fight and the Democratic party was seriously jolted. It would take years for the scars of this campaign to heal. The Republicans were jubilant. Such a Democratic brawl was made to their measure. They could quote Democrats as authority that Democrats were thieves, and they fully expected to carry the state. But President Roosevelt's third-term sweep of Missouri helped Truman win re-election in November over Republican Marvel ·H. Davis by a 44,000 vote margin.

Milligan was again reappointed as District Attorney. This time Truman did not object and agreed to the appointment. If he had not, Milligan would not have been confirmed. However, subsequently, Truman, as Vice-President, vigorously opposed a third appointment. The reappointment was delayed, and later, as President, Truman—honestly disdainful of the criticism that might accrue—declined to reappoint Milligan. In Milligan's place he named Sam Wear of Springfield, a lifelong Democrat, and a man who, at the Chicago convention, had insisted that only Truman was out of order when the Senator sought to discourage Wear's indorsement of him for Vice-President. Truman's record of opposition to Milligan was thoroughly consistent. As far as Truman was concerned, the Pendergast record was only incidental. Truman simply did not consider Milligan to be a capable, fair-minded attorney. As President he ousted him— saying he had enjoyed long enough an office that should be "passed around."

Truman's record in the Senate largely followed the administration line, but rather by conviction than by political servitude. In this record is a guide to an understanding of Truman's thoughts and policies. On preparedness and foreign policy his voting record is consistently and realistically forthright. He is a progressive conservative on domestic policy. His is not a senatorial record that bespeaks either

Senator

imagination or startling innovations of policy though Truman is inherently liberal. He has been the economic and political underdog long enough to have developed this tendency. But he is not a radical. He has never associated or moved in either rightist or leftist organizations or groups.

Chapter Seven

Investigator

THREE MONTHS AFTER THE SENATORIAL ELECTION of 1940, in which Harry Truman had such a narrow political escape, he took the first steps on a course destined to lead to the White House.

It was in mid-January that Truman began to receive reports which were most disturbing to a man who knows the value of a dollar. No one then imagined the ultimate size of the national defense program. There was talk of 150 billion dollars for war programs and possibly a hundred billion more. Grants of ten billion dollars in a lump were being ground through the Appropriations Committee, and authorizations for still greater expenditures were coming from the legislative Military Affairs Committee, on both of which Truman served. Not even the most visionary Senators had conceived a sum of $250,000,000,000. For all practical purposes, it amounted only to a staggering row of ciphers and figures headed by a dollar sign.

Truman was getting letters from Missouri complaining that money was being wasted with a disregard of public welfare in the construction of Fort Leonard Wood. The immense camp construction program was just getting under way, and if the reports were true, it was apparent that millions of dollars would be thrown away before the growing United States Army was even housed.

The Senator decided to see for himself. On a cold, wintry morning he loaded his suitcases into his car, and drove from Washington straight and unannounced to the fort.

He arrived without fanfare and strolled quietly through the sprawling huts and skeleton frameworks of great barracks. He saw men loafing and getting paid for it. He saw material piled almost as high as an Ozark mountain—material that would not be used for months, if at all. On every hand he saw evidence of waste and poor management. He realized that in two decades of peace, America had failed to plan enough for war. He remembered the last time and the wave of disillusionment that followed. He made notes on all that he saw. Then he called on foremen and contractors and asked for estimates of cost, and reports on the amounts of money expended, salary schedules and weekly time sheets and pay rolls. He requested everything he could think of that would give him a clue to the real facts behind this phase of the national defense program.

Truman left the camp with a brief case filled with evidence, drove on to Independence and visited his mother while he rested for several days. Then he took a circuitous route and drove back to Washington, visiting camp construction projects along the way. At each stop he gathered similar data to that he had obtained at Fort Leonard Wood. Everywhere the story was the same.

Investigator

The gigantic program for building camps and permanent cantonments was under the supervision of the Army Quartermaster Corps. Speed was essential and haste was making for waste. But here was such a huge task of purchasing and managing as had never before been faced by the Army. It had not even been visualized and the much-advertised plans for M-Day simply did not exist. There were no specifications so contractors could not bid on the jobs. Cost-plus-fixed-fee contracts had to be let, and cost estimates on projects would be constantly revised and always upward. There was no incentive to save. Even though the fee was fixed, contractors knew that specifications could be changed and that a more expensive job would furnish a basis for a higher fee.

Truman returned to Washington mad clear through. As a member of the Senate Appropriations Committee he had voted to provide these billions for national defense, and now the money was being wasted. On February 10, 1941, he got up and told the Senate about it. He insisted that to avoid a national scandal and to spur on the defense effort, a special committee should be established that would hunt down waste, inefficiency, and open up the bottlenecks that were jamming the program. His thesis was simple: "Investigate as you go along. What's the sense in looking back years later and showing how bad things were at the time?"

Truman's point was well taken. After the first World War there had been 116 investigating committees. Their proceedings were often marked with bitter political controversies, muckraking investigations and attacks on business. All they ever proved was how not to run a war.

It was this realization that prompted Truman to introduce what was to become one of the most famous resolutions in modern Senate history—Senate Resolution 71, to establish just such a committee as he had proposed. The resolution was referred to the Military Affairs Committee and unanimously approved. However, thereupon the then Senator James F. Byrnes, Chairman of the Committee on Audit and Control, laid the resolution aside and the Senate proceeded to think it over. The Administration looked with some misgivings upon this proposal. There were risks involved. The Committee could become a sieve for defense secrets which it could pry loose. It could hamper military plans and frustrate busy generals. It might cause the managers of the defense effort to temporize and hedge their decisions, lest they be hauled up and criticized for their honest efforts. It might interfere with the success of the gathering war program, and could do irreparable harm to public morale.

There was some logic in these arguments, but a logic that failed to give full weight to Truman's fair-mindedness and his own earnest desire to make the defense program an efficient and a sound one.

Truman was convinced that the investigation should get under way immediately. Moreover, his speech on national defense waste had brought in mail from the people, who themselves realized the need for continuing vigilance.

Investigator

It was on March 1, 1941, that the Senate passed Senate Resolution 71, setting up a committee of seven Senators and granting $15,000 of the $25,000 Truman had requested. Truman, being the sponsor of the resolution, was made chairman. He accepted the money allowance graciously and set out to justify even this small expenditure.

It was under these circumstances that the Committee launched on its illustrious career. It had little money, no prestige, the heavy suspicion of governmental departments, and an almost unbelievable task of policing a program expanding so rapidly as to be almost beyond human comprehension. Probably no other committee in Congress was created with less immediate promise and ran it into more substantial recognition and esteem.

As it turned out, greater care has rarely been exercised than in the selection of the members of this Committee. They were in a sense the blue-ribbon grand jury of the American Congress, and the task they laid out for themselves when they organized in the Spring of 1941 in the office of Harry Truman of Missouri, was a monumental one.

The Committee's first job was to hire a lawyer, and here it registered an early major success. Political straphangers with quaint and sometimes nebulous legal qualifications were storming the Committee, looking for jobs. The members delegated Truman the job of finding a competent lawyer, and he went directly to the then Attorney General Robert Jackson for advice. Up in New York, Jackson had a Special

Investigator

Assistant in his early thirties who was earning a real reputation. Jackson recommended Hugh Fulton, who had just sent Howard C. Hopson of Associated Gas & Electric to the penitentiary, and was busy indicting Circuit Judge J. Warren Davis.

Fulton, in appearance, might possibly pass for a banker. The resemblance would certainly cease there. The cautious, slow-motion conservatism of banking circles is a mood wholly foreign to his disposition. He weighs about 230 pounds and stands over six feet tall. His large, well-shaped hands tremble only on those rare occasions when he is fatigued or intensely annoyed. Fear is not in his make-up and his energy is nearly boundless. Coupled with his driving power is an acute understanding of diverse problems, a talent for grasping the essential points, and a lack of patience for conclusions not grounded solidly on the facts.

Jackson brought Truman and Fulton together. Fulton had a lawyer's distaste for investigations that pattern the evidence to get the headlines; Truman wondered if the young lawyer could handle the tremendous responsibilities of a national defense investigation.

Fulton wanted to know if the Committee was going to be one more bunch of headline hunters. "Certainly not," said Truman. "Then," asked Fulton, "would the Committee back its lawyer?"

"You get the facts," Truman said bluntly, "that will be all we will want. Don't show anybody any favors. We haven't any axes to grind, nor any sacred cows. If you can get the truth, the Committee will stand behind you to the limit. This won't be a whitewash or a witch hunt. I'll guarantee that!"

Fulton liked the way Truman put the proposition to him. Yet there were reasons that would have made many hesitate. Here was a committee with a meagre $15,000 appropriation. The chairman was virtually unknown outside the state of Missouri. Even there it was Senator Bennett Champ Clark about whom most people knew. Truman's voting record during his first term as Senator had closely hugged the party line, and the Committee would have to criticize Administration mistakes. The other Committee members were mostly junior Senators, green to their jobs. Fulton realized his own reputation as a prosecutor was assured in New York with bright prospects for the future. His friends advised against lining up with an unknown quantity in Congress. If Truman's Committee missed its opportunity, it would be only a minor mishap in the annals of the Senate. But such a failure might be almost disastrous to Hugh Fulton's career.

Still, Fulton liked the way Truman put the cards on the table. It was a gamble. But it was a job that had to be done. A powerful agent of Congress was urgently needed to probe the sprawling national defense program. Only through Congress itself could an effective check be made on the use of the enormous grants of power and money which Congress had authorized.

Investigator

"I'll take the job," Fulton told Truman after he had thought it all over.

The Truman-Fulton partnership was to be productive of more good constructive soul-searching for Uncle Sam, more enlightened criticism and remedial action than any other meeting between two men in the memory of Washington's oldest observers. Hugh Fulton went out to get the facts for Harry Truman and the Senate. He brought them in by the truckload—statistics, blueprints, charts, confidential files, military reports, catalogues of data.

With Fulton installed, the Committee prepared to do business. Every section of the country was represented in the membership: Maine, New York, Texas, New Mexico, Missouri, Minnesota, and Washington. And as its work expanded, Senators from West Virginia, Ohio, and Michigan were added.

The Truman Committee had to steer a course over many shoals, and from the beginning the members and their counsel realized they would have to formulate policies designed to assure attainment of the prime objectives. These policies were never written down. Rather they evolved and became settled as time went by.

The number one decision was to be the key to much of the Committee's success. They determined that under no circumstances would the Committee constitute itself a Committee on the Conduct of the War, if war should come as it did nine months later. Each member was versed in the history of a similar Civil War committee that injected politics and preferment into the war, drove Abraham Lincoln desperate and harassed his generals in the field. The Truman Committee swore that it would never touch such matters as the selection of commanders, the choice or formulation of strategy, the disciplining of men, or the disposal and use of troops and munitions, and it never did.

The second decision of the Committee was almost equally important. Its members, with hard-headed horse-sense, agreed that Franklin D. Roosevelt was the Commander in Chief, the third-term campaign was history, and that politics should not be allowed to discolor the Committee's work or its conclusions. This was an almost unheard-of decision for a bi-partisan committee.

Its third resolution was to constitute itself an impartial fact-finding agency open both to the complaints of government and business, and to dispense justice with as much evenhandedness as its intelligence would permit.

A fourth decision was to make such investigation meticulous and thorough, to depend upon the records and not upon hearsay and rumor. Complainants would be required to produce the record; everybody would be given his day in the Committee court. There would be no unwarranted, vicious attacks either on business or government bureaus, and no truckling to any man or agency, public or private.

The Committee, with Fulton organizing the staff and guiding its efforts, kept its pledges magnificently. It went after facts and ever more facts. It obtained some of the most secret memoranda from the War Production Board, Army, and Navy files. It took, in secret sessions, production figures on guns, ships, steel, aluminum, reports on submarine sinkings, convoy losses and other data loaded with dynamite. In four years, no real national defense secret has leaked from the Committee, although it has been a walking library of military and home-front confidences.

The Committee, which since the summer of 1944 has been under the chairmanship of Senator James M. Mead of New York, has issued thirty-five reports, all unanimous. It has heard some eight hundred witnesses in open sessions; nine hundred more behind locked doors. It has taken about seventy thousand pages of testimony, enough to fill a twelve-foot shelf. Its files bulge with data that cannot be published until after the war has ended.

About a year ago officials of the Archives of the United States conducted a special survey of the Committee's files. Already rows of cabinets filled with Committee information are lined up in the Archives Building on Constitution Avenue. At last count, the Committee files had been catalogued into nearly fifty thousand breakdowns covering the minutest matters pertaining to America's war effort.

Two or more members of the Committee visited every national defense plant of any size in the country. Truman estimates that he himself traveled more than thirty thousand miles on Committee business, checking production, labor troubles, waste and improper practices. The Committee received sometimes as many as two hundred tips a week in the mails, has discarded nothing that appeared to bear possibilities of turning up faulty production, laziness or malicious mismanagement.

Businessmen quickly learned that here was one agency of government always ready ·to hear both sides of any disagreement, to give both an equal chance, and to consider all explanations, and get to the very bottom of any tangled controversy. This court was always open, eager for business, hungry for the facts, itching to prod up the war effort. Government agencies soon realized that the Committee stood always over them like a stern but indulgent parent, a bouquet in one hand if deserved, a hickory paddle in the other if it had to be that. But it also had a strain of tolerance. It did not nag or take a high moral tone.

When Andrew Jackson Higgins of New Orleans wanted to build landing boats and found himself stopped by official indifference, he got a hearing from the Truman Committee, which resulted in an investigation and the awarding of a Navy Contract.

When a construction company put up patchwork defense housing at Winfield Park, New Jersey, and made a poor performance on the construction of concrete barges, the Truman Committee investigated. The evidence was later turned over to the Department of Justice and jury indictments followed. When steel tests at the Irvin works of the Carnegie-Illinois Steel Co. were faked and falsified, the Truman Committee, tipped by a disillusioned employee, went to work, Company officials admitted the faking and stopped the practice. When defective airplane motors were passed at the

Five Truman Committee members and counsel meet in "Harry's Doghouse." Left to right: Attorney Hugh Fulton, Senator Tom Connally, Senator Joseph H. Ball, Truman, and Senators Harley Kilgore and Owen Brewster. In this small room, many of America's most pressing war problems were resolved.

Courtesy LIFE

America's First Family: Mrs. Truman, the President, and their only child Mary Margaret, spending an evening in their plainly furnished home in Independence, during the days when Truman was a Senator from Missouri. Although Senator Truman was usually busy with official duties, he sometimes found time to take his family to the movies, which he enjoys. As Mrs. Truman explains, "He likes any movie his daughter wants to go to." However, he claims that, if he gets bored during the picture, he can sleep right through it. Afterward, he may tease Margaret about the actors she wanted to see, because he teases his wife and daughter at almost every opportunity.

Lockland, Ohio, plant of Curtiss-Wright, the Committee forced correction and the Army officers who were responsible were court-martialed.

Inventors with ideas of merit found a ready audience with the Committee. When Sikorsky's helicopter was given only passing consideration by the Navy, the Truman Committee studied its possibilities and criticized the Navy for its lack of imagination in not using this novel flying machine. There were dozens of other cases not reported in the press. More than two years ago, an ex-football coach appealed to the Committee. He had run into a stone wall of official indifference and red tape. He had devised a crude means for firing a rocket projectile and had experimented at great personal risk. He had fired his missile for considerable distances and was convinced that with the right laboratory facilities, it could be improved to fire hundreds of miles. The Committee made judicious inquiry and within a few weeks the ex-coach wrote and thanked the Committee, stating that he was getting all the co-operation he needed. This was long before buzz-bombs were showering destruction on England.

After months of fruitless effort in Washington a small California boatbuilder, with Committee help, got a Navy experimental contract to build life rafts made of cork and wood, which he designed to be dropped from the bays of bomber planes.

Whenever these smaller matters came up, the Committee simply asked itself, "Will it help win the war?" If not, it was quickly cast aside. If it appeared to have merit the Committee could not and would not stand in technical judgment, but it did insist on a fair appraisal by the agencies having jurisdiction. Many of the cases came from those seeking special privilege, or from the disgruntled. Many others were just plain crackpot ideas. One proposal advocated that every soldier in our Army be supplied with a single-seater airplane into which would be shoveled a "few square yards of good American soil." This vast armada would then take off, fly over Tokyo, dump the earth and thus bury Japan in defeat.

Another suggestion involved building two huge, steel spheres three times the size of the Capitol dome. Great pointed spikes would stick out all around the surface. They could travel on land or sea and inside were to be huge motors and a complicated system of stabilizers and gyroscopes to prevent the large crews from turning upside down. These steel balls would cost fifty million dollars apiece, but as the inventor said, "They could roll against the enemy, chewing up armies and cities like a meat grinder. Just two of them could stop the war in no time."

The Committee has had its disagreements with the Navy Department, with the Standard Oil Company of New Jersey, with Army authorities, with dozens of national defense contractors, and with rambunctious John L. Lewis. It never came off second best in the public's opinion.

Within four months after it was organized, on June 26, 1941, the Committee made its first report to the Senate. It had made an exhaustive investigation of United States aluminum production balanced against the then current and future needs. As it was to do so many times after that, the Committee pounded away at an obvious truth that was being overlooked by those planning and producing for war. The Committee stated plainly, "Modern warfare demands enormous supplies of raw materials, production facilities, and manpower. . . . For months the Defense Advisory Commission and the Office of Production Management had said that talk of a shortage (aluminum) was misleading and that it was unpatriotic to talk about the possibility of such a shortage." The report was stern and to the point; more aluminum production was a vital necessity.

The Committee kept investigating adequacy of facilities for all basic metals and helped the country realize that we would need vast quantities not only of aluminum but of steel, copper, lead, zinc, magnesium and all other basic raw materials required to build a war machine. There would also have to be machine tools and manufacturing facilities ready to fabricate those materials at maximum efficiency and with minimum expense.

Here was a committee that did not hesitate to report the truth, that gave the people an honest count and demanded results first and explanations or excuses afterward. In this initial report, the Committee served on war production managers an often repeated notice amounting to this, "We are keeping an eye on you. Never forget that. Now get out and hustle." This notice was, in effect, posted on the bulletin board of every war office, factory, and shipyard. The Committee did not attempt to substitute its judgment for that of the agencies responsible. It would merely show up the defects and insist on correction. Its power of prevention by possible exposure was to become enormous.

Many involved or oversimplified explanations for the success of the Committee have been advanced. Actually hard work, teamwork, intelligence, and luck did the job.

The power the Committee was given in its resolution, in itself, was meaningless. Many Congressional committees have had wide powers and accomplished little. The Truman Committee won its power not by the words of its charter but by the prestige it gained by the careful work of Truman, the other members, Fulton and the staff. And this involved the maintenance of three separate reputations. First, the Committee needed the help and trust of the Senate. At any time the Senate could disband it by refusing to grant additional funds or could curb its powers by limiting its jurisdiction. Second, the Committee needed the assistance and admiration of the ever-vigilant American press which if it turned on the Committee could arouse public sentiment against its work. Third, the Committee had to have the respect of the governmental agencies and departments. If these were given any basis at all to protest unfair treatment or to claim hampering of their work, it was obvious they would do so and thereby throw shadows of doubt upon the Committee's motives.

At the beginning, Congress took little interest in the Committee and most of the members gave it passing attention; a situation that was natural and to be expected. Senators normally serve on three or four important committees and some of the Truman Committee members, like Mead, had to ration their attention and energies between half a dozen other committee assignments. Mead, for example, also had to conduct Washington business for a constituency numbering thirteen million in his home state of New York. Senator Tom Connally of Texas was engrossed in his work as chairman of the crucially important Foreign Relations Committee, besides serving on the important Judiciary and Finance Committees. Truman himself was loaded down with the Military Affairs, Appropriations, and Interstate Commerce Committees.

From these regular committees, departments and bureaus were seeking money, authority, power, and privilege. There was a constant flow of bills into committee hoppers, and little time to dig through the mountainous piles of data and memoranda. Tangled up in the committees of the United States Senate are all the vast and intricate problems of complicated and often frustrated government in a great modern democracy. Here in these committees the Senator sweats out his reputation among his colleagues. It was into this spiderweb setting that Senator Truman had to run the circuit of his Committee's work.

It was here that Harry Truman, the Junior Senator from Missouri, showed his ability at quiet, effective diplomacy and administrative skill. He had turned in a careful job in the railroad investigation and he could count personal friends among his colleagues. He now made it clear to them that his Committee's work would not reflect the image of the chairman and in no sense was it a closed corporation. Any Senator was welcome to present cases for investigation, provided they did not involve politics, and his advice and counsel would be welcome. It was a committee of the whole Senate, Truman told them—to keep it informed and to recommend action. This was an unusual way for a committee chairman to talk. But many of the Senators now knew Harry Truman and liked him. They were ready to help him in any way they could.

To the members of the Committee itself he emphasized that this was to be a composite job. They were all to work together without fanfare or jealousies. The serious task they were doing was the important thing. Truman realized that being chairman, he would automatically figure prominently in the Committee's work. And he knew, also, that his name fitted neatly into a headline. But Truman, as the fame of the Committee spread, never sought the limelight. Instead he always insisted that the credit was due to the members and to the staff. Truman suffused his personality and his position as chairman so that the name Truman Committee, known in nearly every household, became associated not with one man but with an impartial fact-finding government group that worked diligently at its job of checking up on the war effort.

Truman instructed Hugh Fulton to hire his own staff of

investigators and get reliable and competent men. Although qualified persons were then hard to find, in a few months Fulton had rounded up about a dozen. This was enough since a small staff avoided the accumulation of administrative and personnel problems and also made it easier for Fulton to keep acquainted with each man's work. He selected his assistants solely on their qualifications, and never once inquired into an applicant's political views. For the most part they were younger men with the stamina and energy to stand the strain of emergencies and the grueling hours which often involved working late into the night and on Sundays. They were also men virtually free of prejudices, outside interests, or preconceived notions. Most staff members had legal or accounting training and broad enough backgrounds in education or experience to enable them to tackle any assignment, grasp the subject matter quickly, take the case apart and find the trouble. They had to know how to get the information needed, without being stalled or side-stepped. Fulton expected his men to be courteous but not to take "no" for an answer and not to come running back for authority. Yet if necessary, records or witnesses could always be produced by issuing a Senate subpoena. The Committee personnel was rounded out by engaging about 15 secretary-stenographers, a filing clerk, and an office boy.

With respect to the handling of the press, Truman laid down a few simple rules. Under no circumstances were there to be smearing campaigns or publicity stunts. "We will give the press the facts," Truman said, "and let the facts speak for themselves." Every courtesy and help was to be extended to reporters, and within security limits, full disclosures would be made promptly but not until all the evidence was in. News announcements would be given to the entire press at the same time through the Senate Press Gallery, with no favoritism shown or "inside stories" passed along. Lengthy reports would be submitted for study several days in advance of submission, and release hours alternated to accommodate both the morning and afternoon papers. The Committee always enjoyed excellent press relations. In turn, the American press has, on the whole, reported the work of the Committee fairly, accurately, and in considerable detail. In addition, many valuable tips have been given to the Committee by observant correspondents themselves.

With the staff organized and the Committee members agreed on their attitude and aims, methods of operation were devised. The Committee attempted to keep the entire production program in focus eight months ahead; where would things be then? This knowledge could be gained by concentrating on apparent or developing weaknesses, and yet bearing in mind the evolutionary course the program seemed to be taking at the moment. For evidence, the Committee went to the actual records in government files and extracted endless masses of data, and sent investigators or subcommittees into the field to do the same in war plants, shipyards or Army and Navy installations. After sifting all the evidence, the Committee staff would brief the particular case and submit its confidential report to the Committee members. After allowing time for the Senators to consider it, Truman would then call a meeting of the Committee in the "Doghouse."

Chapter Eight

War Record

"HARRY'S DOGHOUSE" WAS A ROOM THAT BECAME famous in Washington. A door at the right hand of Senator Truman's desk led into it—a room with high ceilings, ample lights, several small writing desks, a low coffee table, black leather easy chairs, and a couch. The white walls were covered with autographed pictures given Senator Truman from hundreds of his friends of high and low station in life. One wall was adorned with dozens of original newspaper cartoons sent to the Senator by the artists. A side wall was covered with the red-marked field artillery maps that had belonged to old Battery D. And hanging in the corner were a series of prints showing the history of aviation from the Wright Brothers' first plane down to the B-17 Bomber.

Here in this private office, the Committee threshed out its problems, planned its strategy and settled policy questions. Reports would be discussed, with each member submitting his suggested changes. These would all be carefully carried over onto a master draft to be returned to the staff for expansion, deletions or corrections. On major reports, often as many as five such drafts would be prepared before agreement was reached. As was to be expected, some members often felt that the criticism was harsh or unfair, others that it was too mild. But always they agreed on the conclusions and recommendations that were finally approved. There was a guiding truth that made this possible—there is no substitute for a fact, and if all the facts on a given situation are at hand, reasonable men will not disagree on conclusions; these will take care of themselves.

The final stage of a report's journey to the Senate floor involved submitting it, or the pertinent sections, on a confidential basis, to those agencies and individuals affected by its contents. Liaison officers of the agencies or the principals themselves would arrive in the Committee offices and offer rebuttal. Corporation executives wrote, telephoned, and came in person to soften facts, all of which were closely rechecked by Fulton and the staff. All conclusions were reconsidered before final adoption. But the Committee would never modify its conclusions or recommendations unless the facts showed that a change was justified. If there was still objection, the Committee would politely offer to hold an open hearing and accord opportunity to prove the objections in public. Few ever availed themselves of this invitation.

It was also in the "Doghouse" that admirals, generals, factory managers, and cabinet members met in informal conferences and talked to Committee members "off the record." Despite some fears of the military, no war secret ever leaked out, and the Committee with an evenhanded insistence invariably got the whole truth and nothing short of it.

"Harry's Doghouse" was almost a Washington institution before the Committee was two years old, and many of the nation's greatest problems were settled there. When Donald Nelson, chairman of the War Production Board, showed signs of hesitancy in his arguments with the Army and Navy, it was in "Harry's Doghouse" that the Committee told Nelson to stand up and insist that the civilian managers run the war production program.

Following its disclosures on aluminum, other Committee reports followed in rapid succession as the Committee got its teeth into the war production job, learned its lessons, and memorized the picture in its broader aspects.

It was on December 7, 1941, that the Committee was put to its severest test. It was preparing its first annual report filled with criticism of the defense effort. But the sickening shock of the attack on Pearl Harbor caused many in Congress to say openly that it was time for the Truman Committee to fold up its offices and turn back its authority. The twelve investigators and the stenographers and clerks began wondering about new jobs.

For three days the Committee talked it over, then issued a statement in the form of a report: it was going to stay on the job; it had never investigated, and still believed it should not investigate military and naval strategy or tactics.

It would struggle, the Committee stated, to see that Victory was not delayed "weeks or months" by failure to produce weapons and goods in the desired volume. The Committee knew its work had whipped up new energies and efforts in those managing the war effort, that "it is necessary to continue a constant watch for the purpose that (war) problems are met head-on and solved."

The historian may well date the real beginning of total effort for all-out war from the Committee's first annual report which was issued about five weeks after the Pearl Harbor attack. President Roosevelt had set up SPAB (Supply Priorities and Allocations Board) over OPM (Office of Production Management). Defense production was disorganized and a general, indecisive chaos pervaded the industrial mobilization program.

The Truman Committee drafted 190 pages of sizzling criticism and sent them quietly to the President, advising him that the report would be made public in a few days. Before this could be done, Mr. Roosevelt abolished SPAB and set up the War Production Board with Donald Nelson as its single manager. The Committee had urged the necessity of concentrating "authority in one head."

It was a cold January day that Senator Truman took the Senate floor to submit this historic document. Standing up straight behind his desk in the back row, he adjusted his spectacles and occasionally tugged at a button on the coat of his gray suit. As he read a summarized account of the Committee's findings his voice was almost inaudible. He spoke rapidly. It was not a dramatic presentation, but senators on both sides of the nearly empty chamber began to move over to where Truman was standing. Small groups crowded around to hear every word. Already the news tickers in the Senate Press Gallery were pounding out the story for the early afternoon editions. It took real courage to deliver this report. Everyone sensed that. And Truman, the loyal Democrat, well realized the implications.

But he knew and believed every word in the forthright document lying by the little sand box on his Senate desk. The facts could not be denied. They were complete and fully documented.

Truman read on. The Committee demanded immediate conversion of the gigantic automobile industry to war production, the construction of West Coast steel plants, drastic expansion of the machine tool program, better airplane models and more of them, review of defense contracts, better correlation and management of defense housing. It disclosed growing shortages in copper, lead, zinc, magnesium and steel, and demanded action of the managers of those production programs. In plain language it warned of the huge job ahead and reiterated its own realistic stand

. . . the fact that the entire future of the nation is at stake makes it imperative that there should be a constant check to ascertain that the program is actually being carried out efficiently, economically and fairly so that the necessary sacrifices are apportioned to all without favoritism.

Inefficiency and self-interest have always existed. And the haste and confusion incident to war must be expected to stimulate rather than eliminate this tendency despite the patriotic desire to win the war.

War Record

This first annual report was virtually a doctor's chart of national defense ailments, with extensively prescribed remedies, most of which were promptly adopted.

After its first year of work, the Committee issued reports with almost monthly regularity. It branched out into manifold investigations of inefficiency, inter-departmental breakdowns, the performance of finished machines, and the general management of the war effort. In the years to follow, it was to formulate many a cardinal principle. On the spreading out of contracts to include the smaller and intermediate sized businesses it said, "We must bear in mind that even if defense were our only objective, instead of just our principal objective, we would need a sound healthy civilian economy to support our defense program. . . . Great care must be taken to assure that we do not destroy the American way of life by adopting wrong methods of defending it." With respect to labor in general and John L. Lewis in particular it wrote, "The obligation which rests upon Lewis [not to strike] is not an obligation arising by contract with the President. It is an obligation to the United States arising out of the war emergency. It is based upon his duty as a citizen to a country which enabled him to exchange the sweat and physical toil of a miner for the comforts and privileges of a labor executive. . . . No citizen has the right to jeopardize the nation's existence in wartime." On quarrels within the government it stated bluntly, "The influence from above must always be toward unity. Where necessary, heads must be knocked together. . . . Destructive, wasteful feuding must be suppressed." On manpower, "Compulsion in this field should be the very last resort in a democracy such as ours . . . the real strength of any program will always rest on patriotic, voluntary co-operation in making it effective. But it is futile to appeal for that kind of co-operation until a program is formulated." On farm machinery, ". . . farm machines are the 'machine tools' of agriculture. An adequate supply is vital to maintain an increased food production. Before weapons can be produced or used, we must first have food." On shipping losses in the early years of the war, "Ship losses by submarine action have been heavy but . . . not disastrous. German propaganda announcements that these sinkings are winning the war for Germany are not true. However, our own hush-hush policy has given credence to such propaganda. Certainty is always better than rumor. Frankness is the best answer to propaganda." On dollar-a-year men, ". . . the Committee believes that most dollar-a-year men . . . are honest and conscientious, and that they would not intentionally favor big business . . . [but] no man can honestly serve two masters." On reconversion from war production, "Even in wartime, it was the flow of private initiative that made possible the success of the war program. It is the job of government to devise rules of the road, but not to tell the driver where he must travel." On cartel agreements, ". . . such arrangements are harmful in peacetime, but disastrous in time of war."

It is impossible to assess the accomplishments of the

Committee in terms of dollars and cents, and the Committee claims no over-all money saving. Thoughtful persons have estimated between four and six billion dollars, and it has been reported that by its work the Committee indirectly prevented the loss of hundreds of thousands of lives. The camp construction investigation alone, which Senator Truman started the day he drove out to Fort Leonard Wood, is said to have saved the American taxpayer a quarter of a billion dollars. This can be compared to the little more than 500 thousand dollars the Committee has spent in over four years of operation. Most of this went for salaries.

The Committee's record is due not to the genius of one man but to the combined efforts of a group. Under Harry Truman's leadership each man felt personally responsible for the Committee's success and reputation. They liked their chairman and he rarely made a decision without first consulting with both the Democratic and Republican members. He learned to lean upon and trust the advice of the Republican Senators Owen Brewster of Maine, Harold H. Burton of Ohio, Homer Ferguson of Michigan, and Joseph H. Ball of Minnesota. In addition to Truman, the Democrats were Senators Tom Connally of Texas, James M. Mead of New York, Carl A. Hatch of New Mexico, Harley M. Kilgore of West Virginia, and Mon C. Wallgren of Washington.

All the Committee members pulled their weight in the traces though some worked far beyond the limits of their assignments. One of these was Senator Wallgren, a former congressman, and now governor of the State of Washington. He was the influencing force behind many of the Committee's most important inquiries. Unhesitatingly he pointed to the defects in the aircraft program. It was his farsightedness that concentrated attention on the need for evolving new uses and processes for magnesium, aluminum and other light metals. His genial nature often resolved Committee disagreements by smoothing over ruffled feelings and paving the way for diplomatic compromises. Truman and Wallgren became close personal friends and traveled thousands of miles together on Committee investigations.

Harley M. Kilgore was another member and friend of Truman's who always managed to find time for the Committee. A former judge and an intense worker, Kilgore devoted his energies to manpower and steel production problems. He could predict shortages long before they occurred. Frequently it would be Truman, Wallgren and Kilgore who would gather in "The Doghouse" to map out the direction of the Committee's work. Senator Mead would join them whenever he could untangle himself from the worrying burden of his many Senate duties. Mead, like Truman, is a self-made man. He started out as a switchman on the Erie Railroad, worked his way up to Congressman and finally was elected to represent New York in the Senate by a 400,000 vote margin. Mead, the Committee's present chairman, was a mainstay under Truman.

In the Republican ranks, it was Owen Brewster, one of the most astute and aggressive men in the Senate, who gave unsparingly of his talents to Committee affairs. Being a shrewd lawyer, Brewster supplied much of the balance and circumspection that characterized the Committee's decisions.

Homer Ferguson, although he was not elected to the Senate until 1942, fitted the Committee's hand like a glove. Ferguson had made a national reputation by his investigations and prosecutions as a circuit judge in Wayne County, Michigan. The Truman Committee served to bring out his full capabilities. He works late at night poring over Committee evidence. He is a careful analyst and rates as the ablest cross-examiner on Capitol Hill.

Like Truman, most of the other Committee members had served in the last war or else had sons in the armed forces. In addition all had internationalist leanings.

Few persons realize it, but the well-known B2H2 (Ball, Burton, Hatch, Hill) resolution proposing immediate and concrete action to establish an international postwar peace organization was first projected at a luncheon which Harry Truman gave for his close friends in the Senate lunchroom, immediately below the Chamber.

After the Senators had eaten a hearty meal, Truman said plainly that he thought the time had arrived for the United States to move directly toward international collaboration. He sketched the outline of the plan he had in mind, establishing the Senate's intention of co-operating. The other luncheon guests fell in with the idea. They used a resolution which Senator Ball had already drawn up, to introduce as the basis for B2H2.

War Record

They wanted Truman, as chairman of the Committee, to sponsor the proposal. He declined. It would be better, he said, to have himself disassociated with it. Eventually, it was decided that three members of the Truman Committee— Ball, Burton and Hatch—together with the Senate Democratic Whip, Lister Hill of Alabama, should sponsor the resolution. This is but another example of the co-operation within the Committee due, in no small measure, to Truman's own sincerity and modesty.

It can fairly be said that the Truman Committee, with its fine record, has charted a new function of the national legislature in a government of constantly growing complexity. Seventy years ago, a member of Congress could carry in his head most of the details and all of the policies of a rather rudimentary government. Today, employing about three million persons in scores of boards and bureaus regulating, in some degree, practically every waking activity of each citizen, the United States Government is one of the biggest enterprises in the world. It has outgrown the stage where policies and detailed operations can be fixed by congressional debate. Congress, which once laid down policies and regulated them in detail, at best must be content with drawing the major boundaries, and activating policy with appropriations. Yet Congress is still the board of directors. It can demand an accounting at any time. The Truman Committee has set an example. It fixed no policies and did not regulate. But by intelligently using its investigative powers and by gathering facts on detailed operations, it operated as the efficiency expert of the American people.

It was with this in mind that Senator Truman, nominee for Vice-President, on August 7, 1944 got up to address the Senate for the last time as chairman of the Committee. He had sent a letter of resignation to Vice-President Wallace, the president of the Senate, a few days before, saying, "It is one of the regrets of my life that this had to be done. But frankly, under the present circumstances, I am of the opinion that any statement, hearing or report for which I would be responsible would be considered by many to have been motivated by political considerations."

As he stood before the Senate, he was not happy that his days as chairman were over. He did not want to leave the Committee.

Now he was making his last report:

The work of this Committee has demonstrated what can be accomplished through an investigation by a committee of the Congress. . . . An informed Congress is a wise Congress, and an uninformed Congress surely will forfeit a large portion of the respect and confidence of the people. . . . The accomplishments of the Truman Committee (and I am referring now to the other members of the Committee and to its staff rather than just to myself) present an example of the results that can be obtained by making a factual investigation with a good staff. . . . The cost of a good investigation is negligible when compared with the results that can be obtained.

Truman proceeded to wish every success to the new chairman, Senator James M. Mead of New York. Then he praised the achievements of the individual members. He reviewed the work of Hugh Fulton as counsel and mentioned each staff member by name.

When Truman had finished, his friend Carl Hatch arose to pay a personal tribute to the chairman. In concluding he said, "He has led but has never driven. He has been wise, kindly, firm, and courageous. Whatever the Truman Committee has accomplished, Mr. President, is but a reflection of the integrity, wisdom, and courage of the chairman, Honorable Harry S. Truman, the Junior Senator from Missouri."

The late President Roosevelt at one time was inclined to take the Committee's reports lightly. Later he told Truman the Committee was doing a constructive and helpful job and that he hoped it would persevere in its work.

And in a campaign speech at Shibe Park, Philadelphia, on October 27, 1944, President Roosevelt had this to say:

. . . We have constantly investigated and publicized our whole management of the war effort. I call particular attention to the thorough and painstaking and completely non-partisan work of that Committee of the Senate which was organized and presided over by Harry Truman. The Truman Committee has done a job which will live in history as an example of honest, efficient government at work.

It was the Truman Committee that made Harry Truman the logical choice for Vice-President. Yet he did not seek this higher office nor the greater role he was soon to play in American history.

Chapter Nine

The Man

HARRY TRUMAN'S FEATURES ARE SHARPLY DELINE-
ated although he once remarked, "I look just like
any other fifty people you meet in the street!"
He stands five feet, eight and three-quarter inches tall. His
waistline measures 34 inches. His shoulders are erect and
square. Vigorous walking is the only exercise he thoroughly
enjoys—he does it in the regulation army step of thirty
inches, one hundred and twenty steps to the minute. He
weighs 165 pounds, having taken off five pounds before he
became President.

His hair, which has receded slightly, is steel gray and he
parts it on the left side, then brushes it back and down, a
little to the right. His friendly, hazel eyes, well spaced at
each side of the bridge of his aquiline nose, gather up genial
crows' feet when he laughs. Sometimes he adjusts his thick-
lensed spectacles with a quick motion of his hands. He
shaves himself with a safety razor, and when the blade is
dull he removes it from the holder and strops it expertly
in the palm of his left hand without cutting himself.

Truman's health is excellent and was pronounced so by
Dr. George W. Calver, the Congressional physician, less

The Man

than two months before he entered the White House. Blood pressure, respiration, and heart registered normal and his reflexes were accurate.

His faculty for easy, untroubled sleep permits him to slumber soundly within fifteen minutes after retiring. He can lie down during the day, take a fifteen or twenty minute nap and waken thoroughly refreshed, his energy restored, and ready to resume his work.

When he was eighteen, he joined the Baptist Church in Grandview, and he has since maintained an unbroken membership there. He does not talk much of his spiritual thoughts, but is a deeply religious man. His grandfather, Anderson Truman, used to say, "When I hear a man pray too loudly in public, I always go home and lock up the smokehouse." Truman holds something of the same opinion: that little religion accompanies a great outward show of devoutness. He says often, "I have always believed that religion is something to live by and not to talk about." Truman does not advertise his faith, but he sincerely believes in God and asks His help.

His favorite dress is a gray or a brown double-breasted suit, soft white shirt, and bow tie—preferably blue with white polka dots. He feels somewhat conspicuous in evening clothes but he wears them with the same effortless ease he has acquired in wearing business suits. He keeps all his clothes until they start to fray at the edges. His suits are always pressed and his shoes carefully brushed. The habit of being casual and neat in his appearance was formed, no

The Man

doubt, in the days when he ran the haberdashery business with Eddie Jacobson in Kansas City.

Truman does not smoke but he enjoys good bourbon whisky. He keeps a small stock on hand and takes a drink sparingly. The refrigerator in "The Doghouse" in the Senate Office Building usually contained a fifth of bourbon, a bottle of Scotch and often a quart of Southern Comfort, that chain-lightning drink invented out in St. Louis in the steamboating days on the muddy Mississippi. Truman prefers ginger ale with his whisky, or plain "branch water." He consumes up to two drinks, then calls a halt. This rule is strict and inflexible. Two drinks and no more.

When Jack Garner of Texas was Vice-President, Truman served as a member of Garner's "Board of Education." The "Board" would sometimes meet "to strike a blow for liberty" with clinking glasses. Upon occasion when Senate deliberations were over the rugged, white-haired Texan, Truman, and two or three other Senators would gather in Garner's office.

Cactus Jack would look at the clock, and exclaim with ceremony, "Somewhere it's twelve o'clock. It's time to strike a blow for liberty!" It was a simple ritual and put men on their ease. It solidified friendship and fostered understanding. There were four quiet years when abstainer Henry Wallace was Vice-President, but when Truman became presiding officer of the Senate, the "blow for liberty" was struck again.

The working schedule of Harry Truman has always been

rigorous—a holdover of farm days when he arose at day-break to get about his sowing and harvesting. As Senator he bedeviled his office staff by arriving at eight-thirty in the morning, having been up since six-thirty, his regular rising hour. As Senator he would dress and then read quickly through the newspapers while Mrs. Truman prepared breakfast. By the time he was ready to leave for the Capitol, he would be familiar with the featured accounts in the *New York Times* and the *Washington Post.* Later on, after the late mail delivery he would catch up on the Missouri news-papers.

President Truman arrives at his White House desk at eight-thirty. Before his administration was a week old, the White House reporters, who found their lives seriously dis-turbed by such early rising, complained to Truman's mili-tary aide, hard-boiled Colonel (now Brigadier General) Harry Vaughan who served in an adjoining regiment in the last war.

"How long is this going to continue?" the reporters asked hopefully.

"Don't be disturbed, boys," Vaughan replied airily. "I know the President. He'll let down one of these days. He won't come in until eight forty-five!"

President Truman keeps farmers' hours, and his routine of appointments is brisk and business-like. He realizes that in the most crucial days in America's history, he must learn the hardest job in the world, and he proceeds with the pre-cision of a stop watch. The appointment is usually for fifteen

The Man

minutes and it ends in fifteen minutes. This applies to the high and the low.

As Senator, Truman often left the office as late as eight or nine in the evening. Frequently he drove his own car, and it was not an uncommon sight to see him whisking along Constitution Avenue in his light gray Chrysler sedan, with the side window rolled down and the wind blowing his hair. He would cut over to Connecticut Avenue and then on out to his modest five-room apartment at Number 4701. More often he would catch a trolley from the Senate Office Building and then transfer to the Chevy Chase bus which took him to his door.

Invariably Senator Truman carried home two or three manila envelopes filled with Senate hearings, unsigned mail, or Investigating Committee data. After supper, when the dishes were dried, he would spread these out on the dining-room table. He and Mrs. Truman would work together until about eleven o'clock, when the Senator usually retired.

Truman has a habit of reading in bed until he falls asleep. He keeps a small table with three or four volumes handy, and switches from one to the other with ease—without any lapses or tangled memory.

For breakfast, Truman likes oatmeal, orange juice, toast, and a glass of milk. At lunch, he prefers some sort of fish, a tossed salad, a dish of figs with cream, and cold milk. For dinner, he looks forward to steak, when he can get it, potatoes, salad, ice cream or apple pie and, on rare occasions, a cup of coffee. He eats heartily and almost anything on the menu, but not heavily. He functions better when he is "just a little hungry." Truman is not a gourmet; he likes plain foods best—the kind you find on a Missouri farm.

Truman is mild-mannered and intensely modest, but in his public and private life he observes an almost painful rectitude. As Vice-President he was recently embarrassed at the National Press Club when he performed at the piano for service men and members of the Washington press corps. The shapely movie actress, Lauren Bacall, was in the room and was helped up to a perch on top of the upright piano. She crossed her legs and gazed down moodily as the Vice-President played. After a few minutes, Truman, sensing a publicity picture being staged, turned quickly and looked directly into the battery of flashlight cameras. Some newspapers described Truman as looking into the "sulphurous eyes" of the actress, but the photograph clearly shows he was looking away at the time.

Truman never dated but one girl in his life—his wife, Bess Wallace. And he loves her with a deep and abiding devotion. Being a seasoned political campaigner, Truman is inured to invective, smears and partisan distortions. But he is thin-skinned regarding any criticism of Mrs. Truman. If, in the years ahead, waggery or petty gossip touches the First Lady, it will hurt the President deeply.

The President and the First Lady call each other "Mother" and "Father," and the President refers endearingly to his ninety-three-year-old mother as "Mummy." "Mummy" appears not to be awed by her son's ascendency

The Man

to the White House; she writes regularly to give him a "piece of her mind" just as she did when he was Senator and she called him to task for not reporting for a roll call. Truman dutifully answers his mother's letters whenever he has a free moment, though he spares her any undue excitement. She would have enjoyed coming to Washington for the fourth-term inaugural. But Truman opposed the idea. Recently, when excitement had subsided, he permitted her to come to the White House for a visit.

Truman's relaxations are few and simple. He gets his only physical exercise by walking. He has never played tennis in his life and says he's "not old enough yet to take up golf." He claims he can cook . . . "but I've never seen him do it," says Mrs. Truman. He loves to drive an automobile. It is safe to predict that as President he will take the steering wheel whenever he gets the chance. The fact that Secret Service men now trail him and carry out advance patrols wherever he may be, is a source of intense irritation. He regrets the need for the alert precautions the Secret Service must take to protect his life, and the iron rigidity with which they circumscribe his every movement.

When he was presiding officer of the Senate some weeks before the death of Franklin Roosevelt, Truman noticed that the driver of his Vice-Presidential car was accompanied by a stranger every morning. Truman thought the driver was carrying a friend to and from work and one day asked about it.

The Man

"He's no friend of mine. He's a Secret Service man," the driver replied.

"Well, why is he following me around?" the Vice-President exploded. "Nobody's going to hurt me." But he realized then that his protection had become a matter of official concern.

President Truman does not enjoy playing bridge. He reasons that a good bridge player should know from the dummy and from the bidding just about what cards everyone holds. "And what's the fun in that?" he asks.

But a game of chance appeals to him. During the Vice-Presidential campaign, Truman was asked if he could play poker. "Don't know," he replied with his tongue in his cheek, "I have played a game where you put the first card face down and the others face up. Then everybody bets and you turn your hole card up and somebody takes the money."

Truman is a shrewd and cautious poker player, and he still likes to recall the time he took fifty dollars from Vice-President Garner, who enjoyed an almost fabulous reputation at the small stakes table. Actually, Truman confines himself to a twenty-five cent limit. He is too thrifty to go higher. His conversation over the poker chips is racy, witty, and somewhat disconcerting to his opponents. He plays his cards carefully, close to the vest, and is not easily bluffed. He seems to have an innate sense of seeing into the mind of the player who bets one hand and holds another.

Truman has a habit when listening to a friend, of grinning broadly and looking bashfully at the floor. His self-

The Man

effacement is genuine—the plain, homespun quality one finds in a man who credits all others, until proven otherwise, with being as straightforward and kindly as himself.

Yet he has his rough side too. His conversation, at times, is unvarnished and unpolished. He reverts, upon occasion, to the muleskinner language he learned working along the Santa Fe tracks between Sheffield and Sibley, Missouri, or to the army vocabulary of the days when he fought in the mud with his battery mates in France.

Truman has a flair for telling lively stories and jokes, and has given many a rendition with élan and side-splitting gusto. For years, the "Ham and Eggs Club" counted him as a featured performer. This is the group that met every Wednesday in the office of the Secretary of the Senate, just off the Chamber, to munch ham sandwiches and exchange the latest Capitol gossip.

Truman reads rapidly, with a retentive memory. His is not a photographic mind, but rather a thorny one that catches onto certain facts and fastens them there. Truman's brain is not trained to grasp instantly all the fine points or shaded hues of meaning in a complicated report or problem. But unerringly he can think his way through, without hesitation, to a reasoned and common-sense judgment. This marks him as a good executive, one who does not allow the central point to escape by bogging down in endless detail and mazes of circumlocution. Likewise, Truman delegates others to work on problems with a pick and shovel and administer the countless and necessary particulars. This leaves him free to concentrate on the broad problems, and clears his desk for major decisions.

Truman writes in large, almost illegible longhand. Like any busy and overburdened public official he goes carefully over the drafts of speeches frequently prepared for him but usually does not make many changes. Again, he relies on the assistance of others and has an aptitude for picking the right man to help him on a particular task. He places trust in those he selects and allows them to exercise their own judgment and initiative.

Truman's voice is soft and well-modulated with a slightly nasal midwestern twang. During his campaigning for Vice-President those around him worried that his throat might grow hoarse from so many public utterances. But at the end of a 7,500-mile swing around the nation, Truman's voice retained the same pitch and resonance it had demonstrated at the start.

Like most Americans, especially those in political life, Truman speaks in an easy-going, almost breezy manner. He writes, on the other hand in stiffer, more formal language, giving greater form and substance to his utterances. His inner thoughts and convictions are rarely expressed at all. These behaviors of speech are indigenous to America, though they puzzle foreigners, particularly the English who think, speak, and write in much the same language; the blunt, wise-cracking manner of speaking being alien to their precise usages.

Truman is at best only a mediocre speaker. But what he

The Man

lacks in oratorical skill and fibre, he makes up in comforting sincerity that does not fail to reach his audience. He usually reads speeches in a hurried, labored manner, sometimes stubbing his tongue over some of his words. He has taken instruction in speech delivery and has improved greatly, having slowed down and learned to emphasize certain passages more rhythmically.

President Truman lacks entirely the broad education and culture of his predecessor. He keenly regrets that he never went to college. He wanted a university education but there was too much work to do and he could not afford it. He has often remarked, "I wish I had had a college education. I might have accomplished something better. I feel a terrible inadequacy of education."

President Truman's hands are medium-sized, well-thatched with brownish hair, and slightly freckled. His handclasp is warm and firm, but often he salutes his friends in military fashion, as he does not enjoy the role of glad-hander.

Soon after he became Vice-President, he attended a White House function where Mrs. Roosevelt invited him to stand with her and Mrs. Truman on the receiving line.

"Where's the boss?" Truman whispered to the First Lady.

"I think he retired to his study about a half hour ago," Mrs. Roosevelt replied.

Truman took one look at the long queue of guests.

The Man

"That's just where I'm going," he said, "if you will be good enough to excuse me."

Thereafter, boisterous roars echoed down the White House stairs as Truman regaled the President with stories of the farm, of Capitol Hill, and of the old days on the railroad construction gang.

Harry Truman does not forget a friend. When, on January 26, 1945, Truman learned of the death of Boss Tom Pendergast, he decided to attend the funeral services back in Kansas City.

Some of Truman's associates advised against it. The political repercussions, they thought, might be embarrassing and unsavory. After all, they reasoned, Pendergast was dead and he could not appreciate it personally. And the public would not understand the Vice-President of the United States attending the funeral of a convicted felon.

"He was my friend, wasn't he?" Truman asked tersely. "He never turned on me. And I didn't turn on him when the papers demanded that I denounce him. I'm going." He did go. He flew to Kansas City and walked bareheaded in the funeral cortege, and then returned to Washington. The public understood. Truman received only a few letters of censure, and hundreds approved this final gesture to a departed friend. It is not unfair to say that Truman, when he boarded the plane, did not care what people would think. He would have gone even if the disapproval had been universal.

Not long before Truman became President, he was ad-

The Man

vised that a friend's son had been killed in the Pacific. He telephoned the man out in a midwestern town, got him on the wire and said, "This is Harry Truman." There was a long pause—so long that the man thought the connection had been broken. Then came Truman's voice again, "Oh, I guess I'm just a plain darned fool." His heart was full of words that his tongue could not speak to this man whose son had given his life for his country.

Truman is a man whose stature grows by knowing him. Almost invariably, the impression gained by those who meet him the first time, is that he is genial and colorless and little more. Harry Truman does lack color and glamour as we know these today. Measured in terms of knowledge of men and their deeds, in moments of self-reliance, of humbleness, devotion, and tolerance, he epitomizes the charm and strength of Main Street, U. S. A.

Beneath the surface of this meek man, runs a vein of implacable will and resolution. He attempts consciously to avoid basing his decision on prejudice or bias. He listens to diverse arguments, and values all shades of opinion, respecting each man's views; and then comes to his own conclusion. Once this is cemented into firm conviction, it cannot be hammered loose. Here is the man who likes and trusts almost everybody, who is casual and almost indifferent to some things, yet perceives the truth, holds it in his fist, and if it really matters to him, will not let go. This is the paradox of Harry Truman's personality and is a fundamental fact of his character.

The Man

It was this that enabled Truman to maintain harmony and balance as chairman of the bi-partisan War Investigating Committee. It largely explains why in more than three eventful years, with its often being necessary to severely criticize the Administration, there was never a minority report.

One class of opinion in Washington was inclined to give credit for Truman's work on the Investigating Committee to Hugh Fulton, the Chief Counsel. Nothing could be more unfair to both men. Fulton and the President are personal friends and work well together. Truman has often voiced his high opinion of Fulton's work. And Fulton has repeatedly emphasized that the Committee's success while Truman was chairman would not have been possible without Truman's guidance and inspired leadership.

As general committee counsel, Fulton turned in an outstanding record. His ability at putting together facts, in incisive examination of witnesses, and in directing his small staff of investigators, will be recognized years from now when historians bring the war years into focus. Fulton's recommendations were generally accepted by Truman. But Fulton limited his recommendations to matters he was working on. Truman determined the policies and Fulton simply carried them out. They rarely had differences. When they did, Truman did not hesitate to overrule Fulton.

One such occasion came right after Truman's nomination for the Vice-Presidency. Committee members of both parties had telegraphed Truman, insisting that he remain as head of the powerful investigating group. They began to bring real pressure to bear. The Republican members informed Fulton that they would back Truman to the limit on a non-partisan program if Truman would continue as chairman. They urged him to convince Truman that he should stay on. By arrangement with the Vice-Presidential nominee, Fulton journeyed to Martinsburg, West Virginia, and boarded the train on which Truman was returning to Washington. In the three hours that it took to complete the run to Union Station, Fulton presented the arguments in favor of Truman's continuing his Committee chairmanship. But the Senator would not budge; instead he convinced Fulton that it was best for Truman to resign.

Later, the Committee held an executive session in the "Doghouse" as they had done so often before. There was loud, even acrimonious discussion. The membership kept insisting that Truman should continue as chairman. They assured him they could carry on the Committee's work while he campaigned. If he lost the election, he could return as active chairman. If he won, it was then time enough to talk about resigning.

"This Committee has never played politics, but if I remain as chairman and campaign for Vice-President, it will be hauled into politics," Truman said. "It will be attacked and I will be attacked for remaining as chairman. There is no use arguing. I have submitted my resignation. That's all there is to it." Truman had weathered heavy seas from all sides. The best that the members and Hugh Fulton could

The Man

do was not enough to make the Missourian alter his decision.

As they say of such men in Missouri, Truman has the faculty of "getting along." This quality will weigh heavily in the future relationships between the Congress and the White House. Controversial matters, including the passage of treaties, economic policies, domestic affairs, and the re-affirmation of the balance of power between the legislative and executive branches will require the proffered hand of co-operation from the President.

Truman has the touch for amicable relations with those of diverse personalities and disputing philosophies. Senator Burton K. Wheeler was bitterly opposed to the New Deal and Truman was for it. They never agreed on foreign policy or the right trend in Democratic politics. Each respected the other and neither allowed the divergence of view to dis-color their personal friendship. They simply did not argue the differences. When Truman became President, Wheeler was one of the first to telephone and pledge his support.

As a man, Harry Truman adds up into an impressive figure.

Chapter Ten

The Nomination

THE DEMOCRATIC PARTY CANNOT BE SAID TO BE A cohesive political organization. It is, rather, a coalition of minorities bound together by a general community of self-interest which the late President Roosevelt was always careful to stress and to maintain, and which has served to preserve a semblance of unity in spite of quarrels and sometimes conflicting interests.

In mid-1943 and thereafter, the party was disturbed and shaken by subterranean rumblings. Fissures began to open up within the party organization. The Democrats were coming apart at the seams, said political wags, and, indeed, they seemed to be correct.

Southern Democrats, the backbone of the party, were growing increasingly critical of the Roosevelt Administration and its labor policies which they felt established the overriding interest of unions and leftist groups as against the more conservative views of the South. This political restiveness was greatly agitated by the Congress of Industrial Organization's (CIO) bold bid through the Political Action Committee for political power and the defeat of conservative members of the Congress. The hackles of the South rose in indignation.

Negroes, in many industrial cities the balance of power and hitherto solidly for Roosevelt, began to talk openly of returning to the Republican fold which they had deserted almost en masse twelve years before. They complained that they were being discriminated against in defense industries, by their segregation in army units, and that while the Roosevelt Administration gave lip service to racial equality it accomplished nothing practical in this respect. The South was also deeply disturbed and agitated by the orders and regulations issued by the Fair Employment Practices Committee set up by executive order.

That much of the political disturbance should center itself upon and revolve around philosophical, idealistic, and thoroughly honest Henry A. Wallace is one of the vagaries of public life. Wallace was as sincerely desirous of advancing and strengthening the social, industrial, and governmental fabric of America as any conservative; the disagreement was over methods, but it was fundamental.

Wallace's speeches, in some of which he raised—without specification—the charge of fascism against business, and his writings, were calculated to appeal to the more leftist groups for support and enthusiasm. He made many such speeches. He formulated and advanced social and economic programs which in his opinion were in no sense visionary or experimental, but to the more conservative Democrats were interpreted as downright radical.

The Nomination

As presiding officer of the Senate, Wallace in four years had achieved nothing in establishing political friendship and confidence with those conservatives or even the less advanced liberal Democrats in Congress who are powers in the party machinery of their states. He had hardly a dozen close friends in the Senate, and his appeal was not to those men and interests which had long carried the load for the Democratic Party; it was to the more brash new Democrats who had moved in from labor groups, colleges, universities and social reform organizations to take over and make over the party.

The depth of this conflict and its nature is best demonstrated by the Congress' action when Mr. Wallace in 1945 was appointed Secretary of Commerce. The Senate would not confirm his appointment until Congress had passed and the President had signed legislation stripping Wallace's department of all authority over the forty-billion-dollar Reconstruction Finance Corporation and its many associated lending and spending agencies. It insisted upon this not because it was afraid that Henry Wallace lacked any personal honesty, or that he was insincere in his ambitious programs for an era of "the common man." That was just the trouble. Henry Wallace was sincere, and the social millennium he envisaged, and the methods he advocated for establishing it, made the flesh crawl on both the middle-of-the-roaders and the conservatives.

Democrats well remembered that at Chicago in 1940 they had wanted to nominate Paul V. McNutt of Indiana, Sam

The Nomination

Rayburn of Texas, or any one of several other men for Vice-President but that President Roosevelt had literally—by telephoned orders to his convention managers—forced Henry Wallace down their throats.

It became apparent in 1943 that if the President should insist upon Wallace's nomination a second time it would split the party so seriously that it could not hope to win. One of the President's secretaries, after a trip through the South and the Middle West, returned to report that the South was ready to bolt if Henry Wallace went on the ticket. And Wallace, a man of forthright courage and deep convictions, was unwilling to compromise his utterances in deference to this political situation.

He had become a symbol of the division within the party and an agitator of that division. While Wallace was stirring the party turmoil with his pen and voice, Harry Truman was playing a down-the-line brand of party politics. His War Investigating Committee and its spectacular performance in the national interest had made him, in the eyes of politicians, a truly national figure. Out in Missouri where he had once been taken by the rural sections as "another Pendergast man," in terms of opprobrium and censure, it was now being said by farmers and merchants that "Truman is a good man." Truman had kept his investigations scrupulously clean of politics. He had hewed a straight line with his Committee, without thought of political expediency or favoritism.

It was shortly before the National Convention that Tru-

The Nomination

man's good friend National Democratic Chairman Robert Hannegan, a Missourian and political beneficiary of Truman's assistance and support, made a swing around the country. He went back to the White House with one report —it could not again be Henry Wallace. The President received the report with evident disturbance, but he kept his own counsel, even to Hannegan.

Soon thereafter, word went along Washington's ever-bearing political grapevine that Hannegan was actively promoting Harry Truman for Vice-President. To those who inquired of the Senator, he said plainly and bluntly, "If Bob Hannegan is running me for Vice-President he is doing so without my knowledge and without my consent."

At St. Joseph, Missouri, months before the convention, Truman introduced Speaker Sam Rayburn who had gone there to address a Democratic political rally, and said he was backing Rayburn for Vice-President. He repeated the same thing in San Francisco and in a half-dozen other places, and he was sincere about it. It was not until shortly before the Democratic convention in July that Truman changed his support.

Speaker Rayburn telephoned him from Texas and advised that the split in the Democratic party of that state had made it impossible and impractical for him to seek the nomination; the Democrats could not afford to have a Vice-Presidential candidate from a state at war within itself. He told Truman to support someone else. It was then that Truman enlisted himself in the candidacy of James F.

The Nomination

Byrnes of South Carolina, the "assistant president" and the man who, as Democratic Whip in the Senate when he first arrived in Washington, had taught Truman many of the finer points of national politics.

Harry Truman became a Byrnes man, and Byrnes was actively seeking the nomination in the belief that he was acceptable to President Roosevelt.

Just before the convention met in July, President Roosevelt issued his famous letter stating that the field was open for the Vice-Presidency, but that if he were a delegate at Chicago he would "vote for Henry Wallace." This letter was undoubtedly calculated to help Wallace's candidacy, and if possible override the opposition which, generated in the South, had spread through the conservative wing of the party in the North.

Harry Truman went out to Independence, Missouri, to visit his mother before going to the convention. There again, only a few days before the convention assembled, he said that he was not a candidate for Vice-President and that his inclination, if the nomination were tendered to him, would be to decline it. He not only was not a receptive candidate; he was doing everything possible by his own political maneuvers and his public pronouncements to discourage the Democrats from nominating him.

What was in his mind? Normally men do not discourage their nomination to the nation's second highest office. Only those who understand the self-effacing humility of Harry Truman, and his depth of feeling for the welfare of his

The Nomination

country, can understand his conduct at this time. Harry Truman believed sincerely that the next Vice-President might be called upon to take the Presidency in an hour so awful in its portent and so supercharged with destiny that only a man of supreme qualifications should be named for the second place on the ticket. He felt, honestly, that he would not measure up fully to those requirements. Others disagreed with him, but they did not convince him.

Then, again, Truman loved the United States Senate. He believed that there he could perform a real and lasting service. He was acutely aware that Missouri's great senators, William J. Stone, who was chairman of the Foreign Relations Committee during the first World War, then the fiery Jim Reed, and more recently his colleague Bennett Champ Clark, had made their records on opposition to the Administration. Harry Truman wanted to write a chapter of honest service, to the Administration in peace and war, and if possible by this means to be recorded in history as a Missouri Senator whose service was not of the opposition but none the less constructive.

He thought there were better men than he for the Vice-Presidency and the Presidency. He was thinking not of his own political ambitions but of the long days and years ahead, and he was acutely aware that if he became Vice-President, then President, his life would no longer be his own. Overnight, he would be sealed off from his friends. He would become the target of unfriendly elements in the country, the guinea pig of the press and radio. And his fam-

The Nomination

ily life would be completely changed. He realized he might be called upon to play a role for which he felt he was not adapted, on a stage that encompassed the entire world.

Harry Truman did not want the nomination. He tried to discourage it and was sincere in his efforts.

It was with these feelings that he telephoned Jimmy Byrnes from Independence just before leaving for the Chicago convention and said, "Jimmy, I'm coming up there to make the speech nominating you for Vice-President."

This was good news to James F. Byrnes, who at that moment thought he could round up sufficient support to insure his nomination on the second, if not the first ballot. It was with a high heart and no misgivings that Harry Truman took the train from Independence after talking with "assistant president" Byrnes. Had he known what was ahead, he might have remained at home.

Truman had no sooner detrained at Chicago, to begin his work on the Platform Committee, than he became the center of rumor and political intrigue. It was a wild, rough time of Democratic hilarity and gossip.

Sidney Hillman, representing organized labor and the Political Action Committee, moved into Chicago and set up headquarters in the Stevens Hotel, determined to force the nomination of Henry Wallace. Hillman and his followers were equally determined, after sensing the sympathy of the arriving delegates, to prevent the nomination of Byrnes.

It is hard to conceive of a man cast in a more unfortunate role at this convention than Byrnes. He had every vote needed for the nomination save one—President Roosevelt's. He thought he had that, but as had happened so many times before, President Roosevelt, when Byrnes talked with him, had shown an agreeable friendliness that betokened not at all the acquiescence which seemed so patent. Byrnes had been called from the Supreme Court of the United States by the President he loved and served, to do an extremely difficult job. Part of it, as the original Director of Stabilization, had been to prevent inflation, and that involved holding wages in line. Byrnes had done this with firmness and determination. He clung to the "Little Steel" Formula which set an automatic ceiling on wages, and all the efforts of organized labor to move him away from this policy by one stratagem or another, had failed.

Then, also, as a Supreme Court justice he had written several opinions which, in maritime mutiny cases, were interpreted by organized labor as infringing upon the right to strike.

Organized labor did not like Jimmy Byrnes. The South did.

This was the situation when the "Resolutions" or Platform Committee began its work, and the quiet man from Missouri did his best to insulate himself from the intrigue which boiled and bubbled up among the delegates. It was an open secret that Hannegan, the National Chairman, was no friend of Wallace; that he believed the ticket could not win with Wallace, and that his best bet was Harry Truman of Missouri.

The Nomination

Truman was living alone in a suite on the seventeenth floor of the noisy, over-crowded Stevens Hotel. Therewith began a sequence of events that are worthy of a comic book thriller. The telephone rang sharply. It was Hannegan. He wanted to come over and see Senator Truman right away. The convention was to meet the next day, and Truman, since his arrival on the preceding Friday, had been talking up Jimmy Byrnes day and night.

He had even brought along his trusted friend of World War I days, John Wesley Snyder, a St. Louis banker, to pass out the word that Truman did not want the nomination and wouldn't accept it. But, swept along by enthusiasm, and sensing the sentiment of the convention, Snyder reversed his instructions and went mightily to work for his old army comrade.

Hannegan, when he arrived at Truman's room, was blunt and direct: "Harry, the President wants you for Vice-President."

Truman turned a shade pale, his mouth opened and he said, "I told you, Bob, I don't believe the President wants me for a running mate. I don't believe it."

"Harry, I can show you," Hannegan replied. He fished in his pocket, pulled out a note and thrust it over to Truman. It was written in pencil, and it said: "Bob, I think Truman is the right man. FDR."

Truman's face registered surprise, incredulity and some consternation. This disclosure jolted him, and despite the authoritative note and the handwriting which he well recognized, he found it hard to believe. He burst out:

"Bob, I don't want the darned thing."

Then he told Hannegan that he had come to Chicago to nominate Byrnes, and that he was not himself a candidate. That night Harry Truman did not sleep much, and the next day Hannegan telephoned again and asked him to come over to his suite. When Truman arrived there was a group of men including Postmaster General Frank Walker. Almost on the instant of his arrival, the telephone rang and it was the President calling from San Diego, California. He wanted to know if Hannegan had "straightened that thing out yet."

"No," said Hannegan, "he won't work with us," and the President with some asperity told Hannegan, "Well, you're a fine National Chairman."

It is doubtful that the Democrats ever had a more unreceptive candidate, or if a politician from Missouri ever had his feet held more consistently to a hotter fire than that endured by Harry Truman. His wife Bess thought he should not take it; so did Truman. All others thought that he should.

Sidney Hillman, his Political Action Committee battling ruggedly for Henry Wallace, telephoned Truman and invited him to breakfast. When they sat down to grapefruit, toast, scrambled eggs, and marmalade, Truman asked the labor leader, "Sidney, let me ask you a question. Will you support Jimmy Byrnes for the Vice-Presidency?"

The Nomination

Hillman replied in the negative, said he was supporting Wallace. A long political discussion followed in which Truman reported that Southerners had threatened to him to "bolt the ticket if Wallace is nominated." It was a nearly impossible situation. Organized labor seemingly would not support Byrnes and the South would not support Wallace.

"If we can't get Wallace," said Hillman, "there is only one other man we would consider supporting."

"Who is that?" Senator Truman asked.

"You, Senator," Hillman said laconically.

Again, as often during the convention, Truman said he was not a candidate and that he was "working for Jimmy Byrnes."

Later in the same day, Philip Murray of the CIO, and then A. F. Whitney, President of the Brotherhood of Railway Trainmen, delivered the same report to Harry Truman. His head was beginning to swim, and he was fast becoming a badgered, bedeviled man. Every time he asked a vote for Byrnes, the answer came back, "We're for you."

William Green, President of the American Federation of Labor, invited him to breakfast, said the Federation was supporting him and no one else.

The Missouri delegation met, with Truman presiding as its chairman, and a resolution was introduced indorsing his nomination for Vice-President. Truman ruled it "out of order." Sam Wear, the Missouri Democratic Chairman, who was later to be appointed by Truman to succeed District Attorney Milligan at Kansas City, jumped up from his chair and shouted, "There's nobody out of order here but the chairman of this delegation. I demand a vote." The resolution was adopted.

Senators Millard F. Tydings and George L. Radcliffe of Maryland ran into Truman in the Stevens Hotel lobby, and invited him to address their state delegation. He did so, re-iterated that he was not a candidate and that he wanted Byrnes to be nominated. Governor Herbert F. O'Connor of Maryland got up, looked straight at Truman and said, "You're crazy as hell."

Daniel Tobin, president of the Teamsters Union and a close friend of President Roosevelt's, asked Truman, "What are you going to do?" Truman replied that he was for Byrnes, and that he was set against the nomination for himself.

The nomination was being pushed down Harry Truman's throat just as the Wallace nomination had been forced on the convention in 1940. A delegation of Southern Demo-crats headed by Senator John H. Bankhead of Alabama—whose brother, the late Speaker Will Bankhead, had been defeated by Henry Wallace in 1940—called on Truman.

They said simply that if Henry Wallace were nominated the South would "bolt the ticket," put up rump Democrats and split the party into a dozen pieces. If Truman would agree to accept the nomination the South would go along.

"Hell's fire," one southerner exploded, "the man nomi-nated as Vice-President at this convention may be President one day. The South knows that. President Roosevelt may not serve out this term. And we won't have Henry Wallace. It's up to you, Harry, you or nobody. We'll not go along with Henry Wallace on the ticket."

Another said, "You've got to be the Vice-Presidential candidate, Harry. You've got to be."

Harry Truman's mind was in a turmoil. He needed help, and he went to the highest authority.

That night he locked everyone out of his room and sat down to think. By this time candidates were blossoming all over the city. Brassy, hired bands were whooping it up for one man or another, and the CIO and assorted groups were raising a terrific dither for Henry Wallace.

Truman tried to think it out, but thinking in such a noisy, crazed atmosphere did not get one far. He asked devoutly the guidance of God to tell him what to do. He knew that Bess Truman would want him to pray, and he himself felt the awful need of help that he could not get anywhere in Chicago—from Hannegan, Mayor Kelly, Senators Tydings or Bankhead, or anywhere else.

It was a wild, confusing atmosphere, and it was one of the most trying hours of Harry Truman's life. He telephoned John Snyder, got him out of bed, and asked what he thought. Snyder said, "Heck, take it, I'm for you." Truman then asked if Snyder would release him from his pledge not to accept the nomination, and Snyder said with great relish that he would be delighted— "Go right ahead, Harry, and take the nomination."

It was nearly midnight when the telephone jangled clam-

The Nomination

orously, its bell splitting the quiet of the room like a peal
of thunder. Harry Truman came back to earth. It was
Hannegan, pleading again, and Truman said, "All right,
Bob, I'll take it. But I'm going to explain to Jimmy Byrnes
first."

He went to Byrnes and told him simply, "Jimmy, they
won't be for you." Byrnes replied that he knew it and he
acquiesced graciously in Truman's nomination. He had been
trying to reach the President at San Diego on the telephone.
He felt injury and disappointment deeply. At Washington,
he could see or telephone the President from his "assistant
president's" office in a matter of seconds. Now Roosevelt
was inaccessible.

It was arranged—at Truman's request—for his Senate
colleague, Bennett Clark, to make the nominating speech.
Clark hunted up Truman and said feelingly, "Harry, I'm
glad. You've done right. I think your election as Vice-
President will make it easier to win the war and fix up the
peace."

The rest is political history. The Democratic Party on
that nominating night had too many candidates. But most
everyone realized that Harry Truman, the shy, friendly
man from Missouri, would, in all probability, be the nominee. Truman sat under the convention platform until almost
the end of the session. Then he slipped out to the floor
where the Missouri delegation was seated, and was there for
an hour before he was discovered—munching a hotdog
with a generous smear of mustard. It was the first time since

1912 that the Missouri delegation itself had not fought over which candidate it would support.

There was little doubt on that sultry day in Chicago when the convention met—after an overnight adjournment engineered by Senator Sam Jackson of Indiana, the permanent chairman, and Hannegan in order to counteract the power drive of the PAC—that Henry Wallace would lead on the first ballot. There was likewise little doubt that on the second ballot Senator John H. Bankhead of Alabama, a man with the grayish-white eyebrows of haystack proportions, would switch his state's votes from himself to Truman. That would start the avalanche as favorite sons scrambled to ride the Truman bandwagon which had literally run over Harry Truman himself.

That is exactly what did happen. While the second ballot was taken, Truman munched another hotdog. Bess Truman was disturbed and worried. Mary Margaret, sitting with her mother and father out on the floor, was vivaciously happy. The nomination was cinched; Truman had something he did not want and something he had sought to obtain first for Sam Rayburn and then later, when Rayburn withdrew, for James F. Byrnes.

The cheering delegates crowded onto the platform to shake Truman's hand. Reporters shouted questions and radio commentators yanked at the cords of their broadcasting equipment to get in closer to the nominee.

Finally a semblance of quiet was restored. Truman blinked as hundreds of flashlight bulbs lighted up his face.

The Nomination

Then he looked into the array of microphones and delivered the shortest nomination acceptance speech on record; just ninety-two words:

You don't know how very much I appreciate the very great honor which has come to the state of Missouri. It is also a great responsibility which I am perfectly willing to assume.

Nine years and five months ago I came to the Senate. I expect to continue the efforts I have made there to help shorten the war and to win the peace under the great leader, Franklin D. Roosevelt.

I don't know what else I can say except that I accept this great honor with all humility.

I thank you.

Truman went back to Independence, Missouri, for a rousing rally with the men of old Battery D and a rest. Then he returned to Washington and on August 18 called on the President at the White House.

Truman told the President he was never so surprised in his life as when he saw that penciled note given to Hannegan—"Bob, I think Truman is the right man. FDR." The President laughed heartily, and then the two men adjourned to the lawn for an outdoor luncheon. They sat at the southwest corner of the White House, in the shade of the immense magnolia which Andrew Jackson had planted there a hundred years before in memory of his beloved Rachel. They ate sardines on toast, peas, lettuce and tomato salad, pickled peaches and drank some coffee. In the words of Harry Truman, President Roosevelt that day was "keen as a briar" and full of zest for the campaign ahead. Roosevelt thought it was "a winning team," which the Democrats, under his instructions, had picked. Originally the two candidates planned few speeches, but before the campaign was over both were stumping strategic areas with the unflagging energy of candidates for sheriff in a doubtful county.

Truman decided he would accept the nomination in a ceremony at his birthplace, Lamar. It was a bizarre celebration. Newsmen by the score poured into the little town, and all southwest Missouri turned out to hear "Harry" say yes. His speech was undramatic and was not a forensic masterpiece, but its theme was the central thought of so many later speeches—"elect the Democratic ticket and win the war and secure the peace." Merchants who lacked buying sense and advertising skill were oversupplied. Hotdog stands wound up with a stock they could not sell; barrels of lemonade and bottles of pop were still on the shelves. Lamar had a financial hang-over, but it was a mighty celebration that brought out jalopy, buggy, wagon, and limousine from as far away as the Iowa line and south into Arkansas and Kansas. An estimated twelve thousand persons jammed and crowded into the little town. Nine United States Senators were on hand, including Pepper of Florida and Guffey of Pennsylvania, both of whom had vigorously fought Truman's nomination at Chicago. There was no longer much doubt where Lamar, Missouri, could be found.

It, like Harry Truman, had arrived.

Press Association, Inc.

Senator Truman waves to the Chicago convention crowd in July, 1944, after being named on the second ballot as President Roosevelt's running mate. Robert Hannegan, National Democratic Chairman, stands at his left.

In August, 1944, Vice-presidential Nominee Truman and the late Franklin D. Roosevelt mapped out their political strategy at a private luncheon on the White House lawn. Afterwards Truman remarked that President Roosevelt was as "keen as a brier" and confident of victory in the campaign ahead.

Chapter Eleven

The Real Candidate

ONE UNSPOKEN THOUGHT AGITATED THE DEMO-
cratic Convention of 1944—the fear that Franklin D. Roosevelt might not live out a fourth term
or even persevere for many more months under the enormous strain and burden of his office.

It was, of course, obvious that only Roosevelt could win
the election for the Democratic Party, but thinking Democrats also realized that there was the distinct possibility that
in nominating their Vice-Presidential candidate they were,
in fact, naming the real candidate for President.

Stories and rumors were circulating that Roosevelt was
in extremely ill health. And when the President went
through Chicago en route to San Diego without stopping off
to spark up the convention show, it was widely commented
on and added to the apprehension that lurked beneath the
surface of the carnival atmosphere. No man before had ever
served three terms, much less undertaken to carry on for
sixteen years.

Openly, everyone spoke hearteningly of the President's
amazing vigor and vitality, his ability to rest at Hyde Park
for a week end and "stage a comeback," but again under-

neath this tone of optimism there was that same wistful note and mood of anxiety.

Keeping in mind the question of Roosevelt's health, the delegates proceeded with their noisy, unmannered deliberations, struggling not so much to agree on a running mate for the President but to choose a man who would be able to keep the party strong and united and, if called upon, could step into the White House, carry on the policies of Roosevelt, and lead the nation forward until the next election.

Lord James Bryce, member of the English Parliament and noted student of American government, viewed with considerable amazement the phenomenon of party conventions in the United States. But he decided that the system, for all its faults and frenzied manipulations, was the result of a growth toward mature democracy and thoroughly representative of the people. Bryce remarked also that the system was more productive of nominees who were "safe" rather than brilliant. "For party feeling," he wrote, "strong enough to carry in on its back a man without conspicuous positive merits, is not always strong enough to procure forgiveness for a man with positive faults."

The truth of these assertions was borne out as the convention proceeded to look over the field of Vice-Presidential possibilities. The delegates were determined to allow only the right man for their purposes to strain through the sieve of their peculiar selective process. Here was raucous, uninhibited government operating in an open arena of horseplay, bedlam, and bombastic speeches with organ music and

The Real Candidate

toy horns sounding the musical accompaniment. But when the smoke from millions of cigarettes had lifted and char-women had swept away the last remnants of broken pop bottles, peanut shells and ice cream wrappers, a choice had been made based on sound judgment and shrewd political instinct.

Delegates from forty-eight states and the territorial pos-sessions, representing all the varied and often irreconcilable interests of a large industrial and agricultural nation, had assembled. A great influential free press, lined up for and against the various candidates and the multitude of factions and interests it spoke for, added its own vociferous opinions.

A strong bloc had tried to squeeze through Henry Wal-lace but he got caught in the fine mesh of the screening. Four years before, he had been designated. But the Presi-dent's physical condition had been excellent then. Since that time a world war had been raging for more than three years; and also certain new liberal elements in the party were now getting out of hand. This was 1944, and Henry Wallace was not acceptable.

In the case of the other possible candidates, there were different reasons. But it amounted to the same thing—they could not be sifted down fine enough. It is at once a source of astonishment and reassurance that the final choice of Harry Truman conformed so nearly to the particular stand-ards of the Democratic Party and so closely approximated the needs of that party and the country when it was later to lose its leader.

The Real Candidate

In his analysis of the necessary qualifications of an American President Lord Bryce stated:

. . . A President need not be a man of brilliant intellectual gifts. . . . His main duties are to be prompt and firm in securing the due execution of the laws, and maintaining the public peace, careful and upright in the choice of the executive officials of the country. Eloquence, whose value is apt to be overrated in all free countries, imagination, profundity of thought or extent of knowledge, are all in so far a gain to him that they make him a "bigger man," and help him to gain a greater influence over the nation, an influence which, if he be a true patriot, he may use for its good. But they are not necessary for the due discharge in ordinary times of the duties of his post. A man may lack them and yet make an excellent President. Four-fifths of his work is the same in kind as that which devolves on the chairman of a commercial company or the manager of a railway, the work of choosing good subordinates, seeing that they attend to their business, and taking a sound, practical view of such administrative questions as require his decision. Firmness, common sense, and most of all, honesty, an honesty above all suspicion of personal interest, are the qualities which the country chiefly needs in its Chief Magistrate.

It is apparent that Bryce had just such a man as Harry Truman in mind when he wrote these words. He conformed to the pattern even though these were not "ordinary times" as Bryce had stipulated. However, Washington newspapermen in a special opinion poll early in 1944 had voted Truman as the civilian next to Roosevelt "who knew most about the war." This judgment was based on their observations of his behavior over more than three years as chairman of the

The Real Candidate

War Investigating Committee of the Senate. This, with millions of American troops fighting in France, Italy and the Pacific, with the war by no means resolved, was another vitally important fact to be added to the already thick dossier the delegates had compiled and carefully indexed on Harry Truman. Only a man who knew intimately how the war was being conducted could qualify as a running mate for the Commander in Chief.

The nation at large was generally unmindful of Truman's philosophy on major problems. They knew about the work of the Truman Committee and had read about Truman's Pendergast connections. That was about all. Politicians, on the other hand, were better informed. They knew the kind of man he was and what he stood for.

The delegates realized that if Truman should become the Chief Executive, he would have access to information formerly denied him. As President he would also be subject to intense pressure and exposed to the most powerful special interest groups and persuasive blocs of opinion. These influences might serve to modify, strengthen, or soften the views he once held. Nevertheless, the general pattern of his thinking was set—he was an advocate of liberalism without excessive or violent political theories. He believed in party loyalty and discipline. He was warm and friendly and, above all, had an honest, practical point of view.

Racial relations, for example, was a serious issue facing the government. It was becoming most alarming, and threatened as a source of real trouble after the war ended. On this

The Real Candidate

question, Harry Truman's public record was clear. He had never made an attack on any race nor upon any individual because of his racial extraction. He had supported anti-lynching and anti-poll tax measures and voted to invoke Senatorial cloture and stop filibusters whenever strong efforts were made to force such bills through the Congress. He had offered no evidence of other than enlightened regard for the problems of the Negro. Moreover, Truman recognized, as Roosevelt did, that the South was one of the country's greatest problems. If he were to become President he would be in the strongest possible position to effect a solution. His roots grew deep into the soil of Missouri. His family's sympathies had been with the Southern side during the Civil War and he knew intimately the miseries and hurts inflicted upon the state divided in its loyalties. History taught him that after the Civil War the wealth of the West had been largely carried back to the industrial East with the South not sharing in the national development and never wholly recovering from the chaos of that war. Coming from the geographic center of America, he might be able to roll in the missing balance wheel and effect economic readjustments promising untold benefits to the nation. Truman would believe in doing this by improving farms and schools, by raising wages, adjusting freight rates and conserving natural resources. The Negro would be given those rights guaranteed him by the Constitution. In June, 1940, Truman said at Sedalia, Missouri:

The Real Candidate

I believe in the brotherhood of man; not merely the brotherhood of white men, but the brotherhood of all men before law. I believe in the Constitution and the Declaration of Independence. In giving to the Negroes the rights that are theirs, we are only acting in accord with our ideals of a true democracy. If any class or race can be permanently set apart from, or pushed down below, the rest in political and civil rights, so may any other class or race when it shall incur the displeasure of its more powerful associates, and we may say farewell to the principles on which we count our safety.

Further proof of Truman's regard for the rights of each citizen was offered throughout the years he had led the Truman Committee in its many investigations. All witnesses were judicially protected and given a full and fair opportunity to be heard. He had opposed national service legislation because it would have authorized drafting men for civilian jobs; permitting government bureaus to tell a man where and when he could work and in what capacity. By the same token, he was against military encroachments upon the direction and management of civilian war production. "I personally am a firm believer in individual incentive," he said in September, 1942, "and I believe that this country reached its present development as soon as it did largely because there was free play for individual initiative. I don't want government officials, whether selected from the ranks of business or not, determining who will produce and how much will be produced. . . . The profit motive of our economic system, I think, is superior to any other system the world has known. . . ." Two years later he reiterated this opinion. "There must be," he said, "and is, ample room in this country for free enterprise, room for every citizen to have the right to achieve and progress according to his capabilities and his industry and integrity."

Truman's willingness to permit free rein to private enterprise was tempered by his realization that resourcefulness and initiative are encouraged only by application of practical measures:

I am one of those who believe that man's progress toward a higher level of civilization depends upon man's ability to learn and utilize the laws of nature. I have little patience with those who concoct fancy and plausible schemes out of thin air, ignoring the lessons and experiences of the past, and who, because they are convinced that existing methods and systems are imperfect, conclude that any change, no matter how ill-conceived or ill-founded, would be an improvement.

In addition, Truman had often demonstrated his belief that free enterprise and the profit motive did not give license to monopolies or big business. He had shown his inherent suspicion of both, since he regarded the small businessman as the backbone of the country. In addressing the Missouri Legislature in 1939, Truman said:

If you will read history, you will find that concentration of wealth and power in the hands of a few was the fundamental cause of the downfall of the greatest nations of the past. We are trying to profit by those examples. Monopoly cannot exist in a republic, and a republic cannot exist when its resources are in the hands of a few. I am not an admirer of bigness. I have said on the floor of the Senate that a thousand insurance companies, with four million dollars each in assets, are better for the country than one company with four billions. I think that is true of steel factories, packing plants and grocery stores. I want to do whatever I can to help the small business man—the big one will take care of himself.

In 1943 Truman had talked out in the Senate on another issue—the spending of public funds:

It seems that when public funds are to be expended no one has any interest in what happens to them, no matter what his responsibilities may be under his oath of office. I dislike to make such a statement, but unless this body and the House of Representatives exercise their prerogatives in connection with the purse strings of the government, much of the money appropriated will be thrown away for no good purpose whatever.

Six months later he was again complaining, "Whether it be by the legislative or the executive branch, we need more effective management to accomplish economies in Government."

At the same time that Truman preached thrift he had consistently upheld military requests for money and authority for national defense. In 1938 he said:

I believe in an adequate national defense program. I think that the old Puritan who prayed regularly for protection against the Indians was much safer when, at the same time, he prudently kept his powder dry.

To defray the cost of such vast expenditures Truman had advocated in 1939 a sound tax system, with the burden so

The Real Candidate

distributed that the smaller man can continue to operate and take up the slack in employment:

If we could get an equitable, honest system whereby the people who benefit most from government could be made to pay for it, and have our dual state and federal system of government so arranged that there would be no duplication of methods of raising revenue, the tax millennium would be here. Since that seems to be an ideal condition, it may never come. We have to do the best we can under conditions as we find them. . . . I am hoping that an honest effort will be made in Washington to ease and simplify the tax system.

Yet although Truman wanted to see business benefited by tax readjustments, and by protecting and encouraging small business, he had also seen the urgent need for international economic exchange.

The United States cannot, nor does it wish to, shirk leadership in postwar economic collaboration. Our own industrial accomplishments have nominated us as the nation that must assume a position to guide others in the pathway of peaceful production. And our own national needs and economic welfare dictate that we apply ourselves to this work at once. . . . The future peace depends on an economically healthy United States, and we cannot have economic health without a volume of foreign trade above and beyond anything we have ever had before. . . .

Truman backed up these views by consistently supporting the Reciprocal Trade Program of Cordell Hull. He discounted the theory that economic health could be established behind a high tariff wall.

The Real Candidate

Coupled with these opinions on international economic relations he had vigorous and forthright views on international security. He visualized co-operation for mutual advantage as a two-way street with all parties showing deference for the opinions and special problems of the others. Unilateral action, he believed, could only serve to smash any peace machinery that was created. On many occasions Truman had said:

I am just as sure as I can be that this World War is the result of the 1919-1920 isolationist attitude, and I am equally sure that another and a worse war will follow this one, unless the United Nations and their allies, and all the other sovereign nations, decide to work together for peace. . . .

For the difficult postwar period he had formulated a detailed and farsighted program. "If this country can utilize all its manpower to make engines of destruction . . . surely we can use that same manpower to provide every working man with more of the good things of life." Wartime restrictions—the wage, labor, materials and other controls administered by government during the war—Truman had insisted should be relaxed as soon as possible:

These restrictions must be maintained as long as they are required to assure victory—just that long, and no longer. Personal and business liberties, and freedom from regimentation are not wholly abstract ideals. They are concrete realities which enter daily in our lives. They seriously affect our happiness and prosperity. Anyone whose duties relate to the war must keep this in mind . . .

The Real Candidate

We are determined that we will not go back to the situation that existed in 1939 when we had nine million unemployed and five million not listed as seeking employment but who have subsequently been employed in war work. This means that we must be resolved to utilize the new productive capacity of the splendid plants built during the war. We must use them to provide jobs for the men in the armed services and for the war workers. We need and want their products.

Business will have to avoid cartels and combinations and concentrate on producing more and better goods. It must learn to earn its income by working with small margins of profit on a vastly increased amount of business.

Labor will have to concentrate its efforts on its legitimate desires for high wages and good working conditions. It will have to avoid stoppages, make-work practices and resistance to the development and installation of new and better production techniques designed to lower cost.

With his long experience in the field of transportation, Truman had also demonstrated his understanding and vision. He had advocated a national transportation policy, integrating the use of railroads, highways, waterways, interstate truck lines and air systems. He had opposed government ownership and favored open, competitive, private financing of transportation with the government standing by as referee. For years Truman had argued for a national air policy and fully understood the almost inconceivable projection of air commerce in the years ahead. He had said: "It is clear that this kind of transport will lace together the great cities of the world in a new pattern when peace comes."

The Real Candidate

On housing Truman declared:

The housing field should provide a whole, new industry for this country, greater in size and importance than the automobile industry ever was. . . . The tenements should be torn down and replaced with new, wide and handsome boulevards lined with five- and six-story apartment structures of the most modern type. Such structures should have playgrounds on the roofs, where children can safely play and get the light and air they need. . . .

These were the more important opinions and views expressed by Truman of Missouri. Party leaders and influential political leaders, including President Roosevelt, were well aware of this record; far more so than the country, and they knew its invulnerability to opposition attack.

They realized furthermore, that Truman had expressed his beliefs from conviction and not as some others were prone to do, for purposes of self-advertisement. All his ideas were not his own, nor had he necessarily written them down himself. That was unimportant. If he had taken advice it was good advice and he had not hesitated to follow it.

Truman's record was one of honesty, progressive advancement, constructive investigation, sound legislation and enlightened voting. This, then, was the kind of thinking of the man who was to become the real Presidential candidate of the Democratic Party.

Chapter Twelve

Campaigner

NEWSPAPER REPORTERS ASSIGNED TO COVER THE campaign of Vice-Presidential candidate Harry Truman accepted the task eagerly but with some misgivings. He was not a colorful man, nor a brilliant performer, and such drama as would be found, it was obvious, would have to be wrung from an unwilling typewriter with a weary hand. All the signs pointed to a commonplace toiling job without any particular pleasantry or inspiration and not very much excitement.

The campaign opened unofficially in New Orleans on October 12, 1944, less than a month before the election, in what was billed as a "non-political" speech. It turned out to be exactly that and the press thought it was a slow beginning. But it was characteristic of Harry Truman. For many years he held membership in the Mississippi Valley Flood Control Association and had long been an exponent of flood control measures, a consideration of great import to the territory of the Mississippi and Missouri Valleys. Despite its being an election year with an opportunity for making a vote-getting speech, Truman determined to again discuss this vital subject. So he talked about flood control and the necessity for soil conservation, and restated the important, though what sounded like threadbare themes, which had long been identified with the Roosevelt Administration—preserve the soil, stop the floods, conserve resources, and thereby enrich the people and save their substance.

Truman had no campaign train in the traditional manner. Wealthy businessmen had indicated a willingness to defray the cost of an elaborate and expensive effort to advertise and broadcast the Truman cause, and it is safe to say that he could have cast his campaign in any proportions he chose. He decided to do it Harry Truman's way.

He would have none of fancy trappings and lavish appurtenances. Instead he traveled in a combination club and sleeping car named Henry Stanley. The reporters had their sleeping and living accommodations in a car ahead, and the two hooked on to any handy train for overnight and daytime runs. There were three typewriters in the Truman car, a supply of paper, a loud speaker system for the candidate, and a recording apparatus. Truman would not even approve the hiring of a secretarial staff to do the typing and mimeographing of speeches.

Hugh Fulton, who had resigned from the Senate War Investigating Committee to help in Truman's campaign, was the chief adviser. He wrote the rough drafts of the campaign speeches, helped to polish them, and advised on general policy. The other assistants were black-haired Matthew J. Connelly, who early demonstrated an acute attunement to political nuances and public reaction, and

Campaigner

Edward McKim from Omaha, a World War I friend of Truman's who watched over the candidate with the wariness of a zealot, and sometimes advised on policy.

Everywhere along the way, prominent local citizens boarded the train and rode along to the next stop, talking things over in friendly fashion and informing the candidate on their "domestic issues." Truman would listen carefully, ask questions, and store away in his head all the miscellaneous information and various points of view on local and national problems. And he renewed his old acquaintances and made many new ones.

In his speeches, Truman did not attempt to raise political fits of emotion. He delivered straight, matter-of-fact arguments for the retention of Franklin D. Roosevelt in the White House—not for the election of Harry Truman to the Vice-Presidency. He urged the voters to let Roosevelt finish the job of winning the war and building the structure of a society for peace, armed with authority to prevent aggression—one that would embrace within its lofty idealism the great and small nations of the world. These were Truman's political chords. But on the specific issues involved, he struck with the blows of a whip. From the very start he took firm and positive stands.

On Labor Day, 1944, a month before he opened his campaign, he gave a preview of what his strategy would be. In the industrial heart of America, Detroit, he told the working man in plain language:

Campaigner

We of the Democratic Party are not resigned to the prospect of huge unemployment after the war. . . . We have built the plants and facilities with which all of this can be accomplished. Now let us see to it that they are operated. . . .

When monopoly demanded the privilege of junking those plants of World War I—and let me assure you that for monopolistic purposes this was a very special privilege—a Republican Administration knuckled under. It granted monopoly that privilege and many potential postwar industries that could have contributed much to the last generation died a-borning. . . .

. . . The same old group is putting on the same pressure to protect their vested interests. And the party that has always knuckled under to monopoly, the Republican Party, is asking America for the chance to control our affairs. . . .

Today American labor wants a government that can do something. If need be, a government that will do much. . . .

But now a word of warning from a friend. Labor has duties as well as rights. . . . Like Caesar's wife, labor must be above suspicion. You must elect and follow wise leaders of proved integrity. Your contracts must be sacred. Above all else you must turn in an honest day's work every day you are on the job. . . . You do your job, and the Democratic Administration under Franklin D. Roosevelt will do its job. Your job is to produce; government's job is to see to it that you get a fair, square deal and the right to enjoy the product of your toil.

At Seattle, Washington, on October 19, at the height of the campaign, Truman was still talking bluntly, this time on the importance of international collaboration for maintenance of the peace.

Campaigner

Let's have an end to shilly-shallying. Does the Republican candidate still have one foreign policy for Wisconsin and another one for New York? . . .

Can you afford to take a chance on a fence-straddler with a record on foreign affairs like that of the Republican candidate, when your future and that of your children is at stake? . . .

With the experienced leadership which produced the miracle of war production we are winning the war. With that same experienced leadership we shall win the peace, convert our industry successfully to peacetime production and march on to a new and better life. . . .

Also while in the Far West, he hit even harder at the Republican Party by stressing the split over the late Wendell Willkie:

It is under the domination of reactionaries. With the single exception of Wendell Willkie, they have always succeeded in obtaining a candidate conservative enough to suit them. They like their present candidate, and with his help they prevented Wendell Willkie from even being a delegate to their convention.

Of Dewey, Truman said openly, "Such a man should not become President of the United States."

In Illinois he discussed big business:

The Republican Party frankly favored big business . . . but even the businessmen found that the Republican prosperity was phony. Wall Street speculators were getting rich, because the Republican Party let them flood the country with worthless securities.

And in the end, even the Wall Street speculators lost. A lot of them jumped out of twenty-story buildings in the middle of the Hoover prosperity, and we Democrats jailed a lot more of them for fraud. The Democratic Administration passed security legislation that will prevent that kind of fraud from ever happening again. But the damage had been done. . . .

In the same speech he also addressed the farmers:

I say to you that the welfare of the farmer and the workingman go hand in hand. . . . The Democratic Administration will continue to work to improve the living standards of both. . . .

Every American deserves a fair break, and he will get it under the Democratic Administration. . . . How their [the Republicans] tune has changed since the Republican convention of 1944. You may remember when one of the key speakers of that convention solemnly pronounced that under the Democratic Administration the farmer works all day and keeps books all night. He did not choose to remind the American farmer that under the administration of Hoover a farmer worked all day, worked all night and had no books to keep. . . .

The government under the three Republican administrations was too busy helping big business to spare any time for the farmers. . . . We Democrats will not say it is un-American to help the farmer and the workingman in hard times. . . .

Truman kept throwing these body blows at the Republicans, and forced them into advanced positions they did not want to take, but Truman always seemed to be getting there first and that meant votes. By the end of the campaign he had traveled through Texas, New Mexico, on up to San Francisco; then to Seattle, back to Minneapolis, and Illinois; east to Boston, New York, and down to Washington and West Virginia; then finally to Pittsburgh and St. Louis. All along the route he kept demanding that the Republicans come out into the open.

Opponents of Roosevelt sensed, as had the delegates at the Democratic National Convention in Chicago, that Truman might well be the real candidate for President. In any event, for twelve years they had tried in vain to beat Roosevelt by personal attack. Now, they reasoned, they could defeat Roosevelt and Truman by concentrating on Roosevelt's running mate. Anti-administration orators and newspapers turned loose a furious attack on Truman's record as a Jackson County judge, as a Pendergast politician, as a Senator, and charged him with being a former member of the Ku Klux Klan. They conveniently ignored the record of the Truman Committee and Truman's long service as a forthright public official. By these devious tactics they conceived of holding Truman up to public scorn and ridicule, of making him nervous and plaguing him into mistakes that would mean defeat for the Roosevelt-Truman ticket. They succeeded in presenting a grossly distorted picture. But no greater political miscalculation was ever made. The noise of the backfire sounded across the nation on election night.

First of all, Truman was a seasoned campaigner who thoroughly understood politics of the vicious variety. Second, he was equipped with a record that was practically invulnerable. His views were settled and constructive.

Campaigner

Third, he had incurred few personal or political enmities during his career.

Between major stops, campaigner Truman was on the back step at every halt of the train. No matter how few had gathered on the station platform, he would make an appearance. The newsmen soon discovered that in Truman they had an adept, cagey campaigner. It did not take them long to sense that Truman was making votes; not great blocs of votes perhaps, but he was gathering up friends all along the route, friends who would go out and spread the gospel that Harry Truman was a "regular fellow" who knew what he was talking about.

His platform speeches were confident, sure of success in the election, rich in their praise of President Roosevelt, and devoid of attacks upon or mention of Dewey, the Republican Presidential candidate. Truman holds a sound political philosophy that much can be gained by refusing to mention the opposing candidate. It makes more friends, avoids personal attacks, and concentrates public attention away from the opposition. Except when debating major issues, why advertise Dewey by mentioning him? In these little five-minute platform speeches, Truman was warm, friendly, and chatty, almost one of the folks standing at the rear steps. He leaned over and shook hands all around until the train would start moving away. Then he would stand and wave a friendly Missouri departure.

Truman was up early every morning, before seven, to read the morning papers picked up on the overnight run, and to breakfast over his campaign problems. Later he would have a glass of milk and a sandwich while he went over the texts of speeches with Fulton. Two days out, the newspapermen were sold on the candidate, if somewhat irritated by Fulton's independence and disregard of their split-second schedules for wiring in copy. Fulton's interest was in Truman's speeches; the newsmen's instructions were to make deadlines and file speeches two days ahead of delivery. Since there were often as many as nine speeches in one day, Truman's small staff could not always get them out on time. Truman was genuinely frank and candid with the reporters. And when they had difficulties they did not carry them to others of the entourage. They went straight to the candidate, and he did his best to arrange his schedules to suit their convenience.

Evenings, when the long haul of the day was done at ten o'clock, Harry Truman would repair to his room, pull on a pair of cool broadcloth pajamas, don kidskin house slippers, and slip into his old flower-figured silk dressing robe.

He might read the newspapers or pore over a speech. Or, frequently, he would send up to the reporters' car and inquire, "How about it, boys? Let's have a little ten-cent ante!" Then, back in the campaign car, the reporters gathered around a table, Truman would shuck out of his dressing robe, the cards would be dealt, and the game would run for an hour or two. In these sessions, Harry Truman was at his best. His running fire of poker table conversation was convivial and unvarnished. He talked politics, he discussed government and told stories and sought the advice of the reporters. He literally took them into his confidence, and said afterwards that many a suggestion made around the poker table cropped up later in his speeches with real returns to himself and the ticket. He asked the correspondents to criticize his speaking, and they did so without hesitation. They told him his delivery was halting and somewhat stodgy, that he did best when he was talking extemporaneously to crowds on the train steps. Thereafter, there was less of strained effort and more of ease in Truman's speeches; less of the labored preparation and more of the impromptu delivery.

Truman frequently left his prepared texts to speak his conviction of God's will that America play a great role in future international affairs, and on such occasions his voice was deeply sincere:

"I believe—I repeat, I believe honestly—that Almighty God intends now that we shall assume the leadership which He intended us to assume in 1920, and which we refused. And I believe that if we do that, our problems will almost solve themselves."

This thought ran like a refrain through many a Truman speech—it was discussed and re-emphasized at the poker table.

The idea of passing through Texas without seeing his old friend and political professor John Nance Garner at Uvalde was unthinkable to Harry Truman. He wired Garner that he would be through Uvalde at a certain hour, and would be glad to see him at the train. It was late afternoon and the bright sunshine slanted down through the dusty haze over the countryside when the train pulled into Uvalde. It had hardly come to a stop when Truman hopped briskly off the steps and strode rapidly to a big, white-haired, white-eyebrowed old man.

Former Vice-President Garner was wearing tattered brown khaki work pants, a brown work shirt, a battered white hat, and in his teeth he clenched a frayed, outrageous Mexican "cheroot," according to Garner "one of the best cigars in the world." His fingers were dyed deep with the stain of pecan hulls, for he was busy with his harvest, and the palms and backs of his hands were roughened and chapped. He was the man who through two Roosevelt terms had been Vice-President of the United States. Now he was back at home, harvesting and digging in the soil after "the Chief" had dropped him for Henry Wallace in 1940. He was a crusty, salty character, lusty with life and loaded with labors. Here was the man who had occupied the second highest post in the nation, and here was the candidate who aspired to it—intimate friends who had sometimes lifted a toast in Garner's office in faraway Washington during better, more halcyon days for both.

"Hiya, Harry!" the old man shouted. "How in the world are you, bless your old soul?" He threw his arms around Truman and then held the candidate off at arm's length, looked him over closely. Then in a shout, "I never felt better in my life, myself! I wish we had time to 'strike a blow for liberty!' "

"We have got time, Jack," said Truman. "You come right here in my car. We'll have one together."

"All right," shouted Garner, "we'll 'strike a blow for liberty!' They won't pull out with me on the train and take me along, will they?"

The glasses were filled by sixty-eight-year-old colored porter Lawrence D. Ervin of New York, a campaign veteran who years before had attended the old Texan. He swelled with pride when Garner boomed, "Hello, there, boy. You coming along all right?"

"This is fine," the old man in khaki pants bellowed. "Put a little branch water in there, son. Harry, I never felt better in my life. I'm going to live to be ninety-three. I work from seven o'clock in the morning to seven at night. And I've got enough fluid and food at my house to last me the rest of my life! This is good!"

It came time for the train to pull away. They had not discussed politics at all. Cactus Jack Garner, who would only have made such a trip on so short a visit for a few men, hopped off the train. Ervin, at Truman's instructions, jumped off too, with a box of twenty-five-cent cigars, stuck them under the old man's arm, and grabbed the rear steps as the train chugged away. Cactus Jack stayed on the dusty station platform and waved. Candidate Truman stood on the rear steps and waved too, until the old man's figure was a tiny, blurred image in the distance.

Campaigner

There was little of excitement during the campaign tour. Harry Truman, the likeable, sincere candidate was out making votes largely by pounding away at the major issues. It was not a colorful campaign—far from it. But there were pleasant experiences in poker games, stories, straight-from-the-shoulder, honest chats and in the farmer-neighborliness that early sold the skeptical and agnostic reporters on the genuineness of the man whose campaign they covered.

Up in Massachusetts, at a press conference, Truman demonstrated his forthrightness and disregard for consequences where he thought he was right. Someone asked him again about isolationism, and then the name of sedate David Ignatius Walsh, Senator and former Governor, and an isolationist before the Japanese attacked Pearl Harbor, was brought into the conversation. Truman could have avoided this question by stating that Walsh was not running for office that year and therefore Walsh's views were not pertinent to the campaign. Instead, Truman, though he had carefully considered the consequences, remarked bluntly that Walsh still had two years to serve in the Senate, and there was hope for his reformation. This enraged the elderly Senator, it aroused the Catholics of whom Walsh was one, and it jolted Walsh's personal following. The schism was so deep and critical, and so supercharged with possibilities of losing Massachusetts, that President Roosevelt later invited Walsh to his own campaign train and, in effect, apologized in order to heal the breach that Truman's remarks about Walsh's isolationism had created.

Campaigner

Harry Truman's statement had caused for forty-eight hours an extreme embarrassment within the Democratic Party. Truman had not evaded questions, he had not trimmed sails, and he had spoken with no regard for political expediency. Harry Truman had told the truth as he saw it, and sometimes politicians are not supposed to do that.

Throughout the campaign, Truman resolutely refused to discuss President Roosevelt's health or countenance for a moment the suggestion that he might himself become President. He raised a wall of silence against this possibility which had been uppermost in the minds of many delegates and most political leaders at Chicago when they had nominated Truman in July. So far as the Vice-Presidential candidate was concerned, the President was in good health, God willing he would serve out his term, and that was that.

He was equally firm on another point. When, shortly after his nomination newspapers inquired into a long-known fact to most Capitol reporters, that Truman's wife Bess was on his payroll as a secretary at $4,500 per year, Truman frankly admitted it. It was the truth as public Senate financial statements would readily show.

"Certainly, my wife works for me," Truman said. "And she earns every cent I pay her. She helps me with my personal mail, helps me with my speeches and with my committee work. I don't know where I could get a more efficient or willing worker."

The charge, from which opponents expected to make political capital, fell absurdly flat after this frank acknowledgement. The truth was that Bess Truman agreed to help her husband and accept a salary, performing at the same time the duties of housewife, when the strain of wartime income taxes, plus the expenses of living in Washington and educating Mary Margaret, became a worrying financial burden. She worked late hours going over letters, official documents, committee proceedings, and arranging appointments.

Truman put an end to this annoying intrusion into his personal affairs by the simple expedient of ready admission and honest explanation.

There was another aggravation, however, that had to be endured. That was the insistence of local bands at almost every campaign stop on playing the "Missouri Waltz." Truman likes the piece, but he had to stand at attention constantly as it was rendered at crossroads and water stops. When the campaign had ended, the notes of "way down in Missouri" were still clanging in his ears.

The campaign plans, followed through, called for a joint appearance of Harry S. Truman and Henry A. Wallace at Madison Square Garden in New York two nights before election. Wallace was the man Roosevelt had rejected in deference to political necessities. He was the dreamer, the idealist, the darling of organized labor and the PAC. Truman was the practical, down-to-earth man that Roosevelt had chosen in Wallace's stead. The speech for the New York political rally was rewritten several times. The National Committee submitted drafts which were lavish in their praise of the then discarded Vice-President. But Truman made a straightforward reference praising Henry A. Wallace as one of the most constructive Secretaries of Agriculture the country had ever had.

There was no commitment of loyalty or debt to the newly-formed liberal groups which at Chicago had supported Wallace so vociferously, and which had sponsored the New York rally. He simply reiterated his own brand of liberalism and made no direct or indirect appeal to any particular group. Actually, in Madison Square Garden, Truman seized the chance of hitting Dewey in his home state. He went into the question of the military conduct of the war:

Of course, the Republicans say that the war is being won by our generals and admirals and not by the President. Actually it is being won by the hard work and courage of our fighting men on every battlefield and every sea. But our fighting men are being directed by generals and admirals selected by the President, and their plans are being co-ordinated by him. . . . Mr. Dewey has paid the President a very high compliment by telling the American people that, if elected, he would continue the chiefs of staff selected by the President. That action recognizes the superb job done by the President to date.

But we can not trust Mr. Dewey to keep hands off, for only a short time after he announced his intention to continue the chiefs of staff, Mr. Dewey, without consulting them and without knowing their plans—or the problems they faced—publicly stated that the supreme command in the Pacific should be given to a particular general. [MacArthur] Maybe that was only campaign oratory to curry the votes of the General's friends, but it was alarming evidence of a willingness to make reckless and uninformed decisions with respect to the conduct of the most terrible war in history. . . .

And Truman spoke again about isolation:

Step by step Mr. Dewey has been forced to abandon the isolationist sentiments he expressed in 1940 and to agree with most of the policies determined by the President. Aside from the fact that it is better to follow the leader who had the courage and vision to blaze the trail, we must remember that Mr. Dewey had to be bludgeoned into giving lip service to the President's program, because he knew that the people demanded it. . . . We need a President who speaks from conviction and not from expediency.

After final speeches in West Virginia, Pittsburgh, and St. Louis to strengthen local tickets, Truman arrived in Independence to spend election night with his mother while he listened to the voting returns. That night, a little later than usual, he retired, realizing that he had been elected to the nation's second highest office—the office he had not wanted and had not sought.

Chapter Thirteen

Vice-President

INAUGURAL DAY IN WASHINGTON ON JANUARY 20, 1945, was wet and raw and chilly, the streets slick with a slow-falling rain. Many Congressmen who sat directly in front of the White House portico where the fourth term oath was administered to Franklin Delano Roosevelt remarked upon returning to the Capitol that the President seemed thin and strained. Several times he had gestured impatiently to those around him, and had flung aside nervously the blue navy cape that was draped around his shoulders.

There was a small luncheon after the ceremonies, but soon thereafter, Truman excused himself and accepted a ride to the Capitol with the Senate Sergeant-at-Arms, Wall Doxey of Mississippi. When he returned to his desk, the office was deserted except for two stenographers who were typing letters. He picked up the telephone and placed a call to his mother in Grandview:

"Hello, Mummy, did you listen to the radio?" Truman asked.

"Yes," the aged woman answered. "I heard all of it. Now, Harry, you behave yourself up there! You behave yourself."

Vice-President

"I will."

The Vice-President embarked upon his new official duties with seriousness and hopefulness.

The relationship between the White House and Congress had deteriorated to an alarming degree. The President sometimes for weeks failed to consult Congressional leaders or to advise with them on legislative programs. There had been one tremendous episode in February 1944, when Alben W. Barkley, the Majority Leader, broke openly with the President and bitterly denounced the Chief Executive's scathing and unfair veto message returning a defense tax bill. The veto had been overridden; Barkley had resigned in protest against the White House action, and was immediately re-elected unanimously by Democratic Senators whose mind was well spoken by Texas' Tom Connally when he cried, "Make way for liberty."

Congress and the White House operated under an armistice rather than in a spirit of understanding and co-operation. Members of Congress complained bitterly that they were ill-informed on policy or developments. The President was so engrossed with the conduct of the war that he spent little time on domestic issues, leaving that job to James F. Byrnes without delegation of sufficient authority to cope with problems as they arose. The President seldom saw members of Congress. He was hermetically sealed off, as it were, from the national legislature, and such liaison as existed was inadequate and cursory.

Only the President could speak with finality on many

problems, and his voice was silent. It was impossible to reach him, and the advice and counsel of James F. Byrnes or any of the Presidential secretaries had often to be given with the qualification that even they did not know what was in the President's mind or what his plans were. They could not speak with authority, nor could they inform Congress accurately, because there were many things known only to the President or his closest military and civilian advisers. It was impossible for them to call in the Chief Executive to help iron out political friction in the Congress. Distrust of the President, rumors as to his health, thrusts at the men around him were spreading like evil weeds.

Harry Truman embarked on the Vice-Presidency with a sincere desire to cure this noxious condition. The Government of the United States—the co-operation between the White House and Congress—was distinctly unhealthy. On those fairly rare occasions when the leaders of Congress visited the President, he did most of the talking, and only stouthearted men, like Speaker Sam Rayburn of Texas, ventured to debate policy with Roosevelt.

Truman explained to Senators, and to his close friends among the newsmen, that his aim was to bring about a better working arrangement between the two branches, to forestall if possible the great storm charging the atmosphere between the two and destined to burst almost the instant the war was won, when Congress should move to recapture the tremendous powers it has surrendered for the prosecution of the war.

Vice-President

Truman wanted and hoped to interpret and explain the executive policies and plans to the Senators—if necessary defend them—and always to try and prevent misinterpretation. Truman even wanted to be an ex-officio member of Senate committees without a vote. With his wide knowledge of Senate affairs he could have rendered invaluable service. And he desired also to analyze and gauge for the President the mood, the thoughts, and the intentions of the Senate. In this manner, by acting as an adviser-plenipotentiary between the two branches, he believed he could bring about co-operation and understanding where it was most needed. But he could only do this if he had the President's full confidence and was constantly consulted on his plans and problems. Then by frank and friendly discussions in quiet, informal sessions with other Senators he could supply the link that had long been missing in the relationship between Congress and the President. He could not take the floor and debate issues. The office he held prevented that.

Truman did attend cabinet sessions on several occasions, but they dealt mostly with departmental reports and were not generally fruitful of discussions which could guide him in his job of tempering the minds of the Senators. Henry Wallace as Vice-President had attended cabinet sessions regularly, but he had made no large group of friends in the Senate. He was received with a reserve that accentuated his own personal shyness, and if he knew much of departmental doings or policy he made little or no effort to explain them to members of the Senate. Liaison and understanding had deteriorated during his four-year term as the Senate's presiding officer.

It is a peculiarity of the United States government that the officer next in succession to the Presidency is comparatively insulated from that high office which he must assume upon the death of the President. There is little in the duties of the Vice-President as the mere presiding officer of the Senate that equips him for succession to the Presidency. He is neither of the legislative branch nor the executive; his burden of routine duties as the Senate's presiding officer gives him little time to study the work of governmental departments, or their policies, other than the points he picks up ruling over the debate on the Senate floor. Seldom is he taken fully into the confidence of the executive. He is left, rather, to shift for himself and in case of the death of the President he must accede to that office comparatively unschooled in its problems and official secrets.

Harry Truman had hoped to bring something of a marriage of minds between the Senate and the White House. Instead, he found that as Vice-President he was expected to attend social functions as a sort of traveling, wining and dining ambassador of the White House, and the invitations poured in upon him and Bess Truman in an avalanche. All the embassies, most of the Senators, the leading social families struck off invitations to the Trumans, loaded up the sideboards with liquors and canapes and prepared for festivities. Harry Truman and Bess Truman did their gracious best. On some nights there were as many as three cocktail parties and a dinner party, and seldom a morning passed that Washingtonians did not find on the social page a report that the evening before the Trumans had attended a dinner as guests of honor, or a cocktail party or a reception or a concert. It was a wearying, unbroken round of gold service and gilt braid and small talk. Had the Vice-President accepted the drinks proffered him he would have lapsed into dipsomania within days, for not even the hardiest constitution could withstand Washington's liquor closets pouring at their tidal best. He formed a habit of accepting a drink, taking a sip, and then carrying it in his hand for the rest of the evening, or until he and Mrs. Truman could gracefully bid their hosts good evening and proceed to the next engagement.

Truman had assumed his social obligations largely because he knew that he could learn from the important people he would meet, particularly members of the diplomatic corps stationed in Washington. Just as he had studied the thinking and the behavior of the Senators during his first term, now his mind swept up whatever information it could gather from the frequently authoritative and usually uninhibited conversation that flowed in a copious tide whenever the party hour arrived. Business and political talks, hints of impending events in other countries, and even bits of gossip about embassy officials were all filed neatly away for future reference.

But the social regimen interfered seriously with his studies and placed a heavy strain on the home. He seldom had an opportunity to scatter the dining-room table with committee hearings and departmental reports and search through them for information needed if he were to discharge fully the responsibilities he believed attached to his office.

After no more than two months of this social whirl, Vice-President Truman confided that it was becoming a boresome, deadly grind; that he felt he had learned all he could and he was being swamped not because he was Harry Truman from Lamar, Missouri, but because having the Vice-President to table amounted to something of a social tour de force in Washington. He was hunting desperately for some means whereby he could taper off drastically on his social engagements and enlarge his own work schedule— the work he wanted to do and felt he should do—accordingly.

He said that he felt that he was not elected a social lion, nor was it his job to be one. And he planned to begin accepting fewer and fewer invitations, limiting his social activities only to those diplomatic and state affairs which it was imperative that he attend. He much preferred to hold open house in his richly appointed office just off the Senate reading room, where he kept the fireplace acrackle with burning logs. Here he received, when not presiding in the Chamber a dozen steps away, an almost steady procession of delegations inviting him to make speeches, write magazine articles, award diplomas; or Senators dropped in to discuss Senate business and exchange confidences. At such times, Harry Truman was at his best. His military aide, Colonel

Vice-President

Harry H. Vaughan, his old companion of war days, acted as receptionist and host in the absence of the Vice-President. He was an expert "strainer" who culled out of the callers all crackpots and the scores of unwanted visitors whose purposes were to load the Vice-President with some chore by pleading for all sorts of favors.

Soon after Truman became Vice-President, the mailbags carried into his office were bulging. Many of these letters were written by frantic wives, mothers, or sweethearts pleading that he "get John out of the Army."

The Vice-President adopted an inflexible rule: never to bring any pressure to obtain the release of a military man. The war, as he well knew, was not won. It had still to be fought and it could best be prosecuted to a victorious conclusion without political interference. Harry Vaughan answered all such letters over his own—not the Vice-President's—signature. He would advise the family to make affidavits of its hardship, send these to the soldier, and let him make application for discharge to his commanding officer in the usual way. Truman did not interfere with the military, and he left to Colonel Vaughan the responsibility of handling these hundreds of requests as politely and informally as was possible.

The rapprochement which Truman had so hopefully planned to foster between the Executive and Congress was rudely jolted at the very outset, and the Vice-President did his best to repair the damage caused by a maneuver of which he was not forewarned and about which he was not even consulted. Two days before the inauguration on Saturday, he had chatted with Henry A. Wallace, the retiring Vice-President, and gave Wallace every opportunity to advise him of the cabinet appointment Wallace would request and undoubtedly receive from the President. The retiring Vice-President was, as usual, shyly uncommunicative and reticent. He told Harry Truman nothing.

On Sunday, the day after the inaugural ceremonies, President Roosevelt left Washington to proceed to the Yalta Conference, but not until he had rocked the city by his curt dismissal of Jesse Jones of Texas from the cabinet position of Secretary of Commerce. As Mr. Roosevelt's dismissal letter, released by Jones, disclosed, the change was made because Henry Wallace, who had long feuded with the Secretary, desired the cabinet post, felt he could fill it, and because of his campaign support in 1944 was entitled to it as a matter of political reward. In 1940, Congress, with the President's approval, had passed a bill allowing Jones to hold both the Secretaryship of Commerce and the post of Federal Loan Administrator, thereby retaining his influence and direction over the Reconstruction Finance Corporation and dozens of other agencies equipped and authorized to award tens of billions of dollars in loans. Jones had retained both jobs, and it was now proposed to march him off the plank and install Henry Wallace in these positions.

Hardly anything could have more enraged the conservatives of Congress. There was no warning of the move, though Washington had been alive and crawling with ru-

mors that centered on Wallace. Jesse Jones was popular
with Congress. He had dealt with it for thirteen years, and
he thought in the conservative terms of many of the most
powerful Senators—men like Walter George of Georgia,
Josiah Bailey of North Carolina, Tom Connally of Texas,
and Republicans Robert Taft of Ohio and Arthur H. Vandenberg of Michigan.

This state of affairs disturbed Truman's sense of orderly
procedure. Moreover, he would not stand by and see the
wedge of discord driven deeper into the vitals of the Democratic Party. He decided he would try and mend the breach
by personal appeal and by advising the Democratic National Committee where to apply pressure and how on certain Senators. He knew that he was beaten before he started,
and largely because he had no forewarning, because the dismissal of Jones was done in such a manner as he himself
would have advised against. Its bluntness had prejudiced
Wallace's entire case in the Senate. For weeks the controversy swirled through the Senate. Walter George introduced a bill divesting the Secretary of Commerce of control
of the governmental lending agencies. Then the Senate decided to withhold confirmation until Roosevelt—then in
Yalta—signed the bill into law. Bailey of North Carolina,
chairman of the Commerce Committee which reported ad-
versely on Wallace's nomination for Secretary, had almost
upset the Administration. Harry Truman had talked for
nearly two hours one night with Senator Bailey, pleading
with him to allow the passage of the George Bill and not

attempt first to pressure a vote on Wallace's confirmation. Truman had advised this as the only Administration course. Only six times in history had the Senate rejected cabinet nominations, most of these occurring seventy-five years before. Yet there was no doubt that in its present temper, the Senate, if forced to vote first on Wallace's confirmation, would reject it. And Bailey was adamant. Nothing would jar his determination to beat Wallace by getting a vote ahead of the George Bill.

Truman and the Senate leaders then shifted tactics. They began rounding up votes to beat Bailey's attempt to force first an executive session for a vote on Wallace's nomination. When the day arrived, Bailey insisted upon making his motion for the Senate to resolve into executive session and consider the nomination. The vote was a tie, forty-two to forty-two, and the motion was defeated. Robert Taft of Ohio quickly changed his vote to the negative—in order to be able to move for a reconsideration, with the hope and expectation that some votes could be picked up against Wallace on the reconsideration roll call.

Majority Leader Barkley, an adroit parliamentarian, was on his feet and instantly moved for the consideration of the George Bill. Taft protested, saying the reconsideration had to come first but Truman ruled that he had yielded the floor. Later that day Barkley waved a slip of paper and then read it. It was a message relayed from the President stating he would sign the measure. The George Bill was passed, eventually signed, and Wallace was confirmed as Secretary of Commerce without control over the lending agencies.

The appointment of Aubrey Williams as head of the Rural Electrification Administration raised another storm in the Senate, immediately after the battle over Henry Wallace had subsided. Again the conservatives were in an uproar, and although Truman had no advance warning of the appointment, and no chance to advise that it would raise a tempest in the Senate, he went to work to organize support for Williams' confirmation. But this could not be done and Williams was rejected. The understanding which Truman had hoped to effect, and the co-operation for which he had strained, both were at low tide.

Truman did succeed in one great effort at rapprochement. Immediately after the President's return from the Yalta Conference, he got in touch with the White House and earnestly advised that President Roosevelt appear before Congress and report in person on the crucial negotiations. He advocated it for a multiplicity of reasons: first, there were the recurrent rumors that the President was dying, that he was ill and distrait and incapacitated, rumors fanned to a fury by the death of Presidential Aide Edwin M. Watson on the return trip. Second, there were the wild rumors of secret deals and allied enmities occurring at Yalta. Third, the eve of victory over Germany was almost at hand, the peace treaty would have to be submitted for ratification by a two-thirds vote of the Senate, and it was imperative that the President make some gesture of official friendliness and understanding toward that body without which no plans or negotiations of the Executive could be consummated into permanent international commitments.

The Senate could make or break Franklin D. Roosevelt just as it had, twenty-five years before, broken Woodrow Wilson. It was time for a showing of friendliness and consideration by the President, and in making it, the President could do much to scotch the waves of rumors that were agitating Washington and the country.

Truman did not talk personally to Mr. Roosevelt about this proposal; the President was virtually inaccessible, engrossed with the conduct of the war and his plans for peace. But the Vice-President did talk earnestly to James F. Byrnes and to the White House secretariat. President Roosevelt agreed, and on March 1, he delivered his report to Congress.

It was not a great report. It told nothing new. It was an admission that many differences between the Allied powers were compromised at Yalta, some in a way that was not wholly satisfactory. The effect of the report on the nation, however, was good. The President was alive and active. The Yalta Agreements did not wholly compromise the high idealism of America. They seemed to be the best obtainable, and gave promise of better future understandings.

What Harry Truman must have felt as he sat on the raised marble dais back of the President, with Speaker Sam Rayburn of the House, he never said publicly. But that day he knew instinctively that a mountain of responsibility must inevitably fall on his own square shoulders. To the acute observer, it was apparent that Congress and the world were not only witnessing a report on the Yalta Conference; they were watching the last tremendous acts of a gigantic man. He had abandoned the torturing steel leg braces that enabled him to stand, and addressed the Congress from a chair after being wheeled into the Chamber. The once resonant voice—which the Latin Americans poetically called "the tenor of the air waves"—midway in the speech faltered, thickened almost to indistinctness, then finally cleared. The skin was an unhealthy color despite the sun and freshness of his recent sea voyage—a trip which in times past would have served to reinvigorate and restore. The hands, once sure and certain—hands that did not hesitate to grasp the throttle of the most complicated machinery with every confidence of running it safely and aright—trembled.

Harry Truman, Vice-President, the deeply sincere and singularly unmarked man, had often prayed in the quiet of his home for God to sustain and strengthen the President and carry him through the great responsibilities and task upon which he had embarked the nation. He wanted Roosevelt to finish the job, and in the days following the report to Congress on March 1, he sought again and again the highest help for the President.

Truman curtailed drastically his own social activities, and began to devote his energies almost exclusively to his work. In the quiet of his modest apartment, sometimes at one o'clock in the morning, he did some of the hardest thinking he had ever done in his life. Harry Truman was not back on the front line of firing again, but he was moving up, just as he had moved into the Vosges, to St. Mihiel, to the Argonne, to Verdun.

Truman knew, perhaps better than anyone in Washington, that any President must have the friendly assistance of Congress. He knew intimately every detail of how a rebellious, revolutionary Congress working under the brutal lash of Thaddeus Stevens had wrecked and ruined the administration of Andrew Johnson after the Civil War, and reduced to nothing the high ideals which Abraham Lincoln had held for a just peace that would heal the tremendous economic, physical and social wounds inflicted upon a devastated South—wounds that even yet were mentioned in Congressional debate and reflected in the struggle over legislation.

Truman had supported Speaker Sam Rayburn for the Vice-Presidency, and switched to Byrnes only after Rayburn had withdrawn from any hope or attempt to obtain the nomination. He felt that here in this rugged Texas rancher, a man of common sense and unvarnished honesty, was a person whose judgment he could trust, whose advice he could seek honestly and openly, and whose desire was above all other things to help. Sam Rayburn had often sacrificed himself for the Roosevelt Administration, yielding his own political hopes for the good of the Democratic Party. He was a gentleman of courage and judgment, and Harry Truman wanted his advice, trusted it, and felt that he needed it. Back in 1918 when Harry Truman was a captain, and later while his deepest cares were the hay crop rotting in the field under a heavy Missouri rain, Sam Rayburn was a member of Congress and performing ably and honestly in the affairs of the nation. He was equipped by long experience and intimate knowledge of both the affairs and officials of government to render sage advice.

Sam Rayburn could help.

The Speaker also maintains a small office affectionately called the "Board of Education," the institution started by former Vice-President Garner. The telephone number is restricted, given out only to intimate friends. Here, the Speaker gathers his intimate friends and advisers. The talk is personal, direct and unembellished by such terms as "Mr. Speaker" or "Mr. President." Here it is "Sam" and "Harry." The conversation is open, and the rule is that such meetings are unalterably "off the record." No one has yet violated the Speaker's hospitality or his trust by carrying from this inner sanctum reports of the conversations indulged or the ideas exchanged there.

Vice-President Truman turned to the man he respected and trusted, Speaker Rayburn—the man whose personal appeal to members of the House is a legend of effectiveness.

"I'm going over to the 'Board of Education' and talk to Sam Rayburn," Truman often said during his short Vice-Presidency.

To a friend who met him in the Capitol one day, he remarked, "You notice I'm going over to Sam's." It was his way of doing things. The Vice-President outranks the

Vice-President

Speaker but Truman did not consider that entitled him to summon Rayburn—far from it. He would pay the call and ask counsel.

These two men further cemented their friendship. They met often in the "Board of Education," and Sam Rayburn invited in friends from the House that they might know and understand the mild, earnest man who might one day be President.

It was with Sam Rayburn that Truman had gone on his only fishing excursion while Vice-President—an outing that might have ended in tragedy.

Together with the Speaker and a small party, Truman went to a little lake in eastern Maryland to spend the week end, casting for bass. It was early spring and the Vice-President rowed while the others fished, for he liked the muscular exercise but cared little for catching the hard-striking fish that hit the bait in a flash and fight with frenzy to escape the hook. Instead, he joked with his companions about their having a $15,000-a-year oarsman.

Truman did not wet a line that day. Returning, the party had to row up a swift-flowing river. Truman was tired of working the oars and stood up to change seats with the Negro boatman. The boat rocked heavily. Truman lost his balance and fell with a splash into twelve feet of icy water. In falling, he grabbed the side of the boat with one hand, but his head went completely below the surface.

When the others helped him back into the boat, Truman laughed heartily. "You just go on and catch the fish, Sam," he remarked as he wrapped up in a blanket, "and I'll do the swimming!"

Harry Truman felt that he had not achieved the full possibilities of the Vice-Presidency. He had fallen short of the great objective which he set for himself of bringing the legislative and executive minds into tune because he could not get all the co-operation he needed. He could detect raucously discordant notes, and they jarred him as much as to hear a Beethoven sonata grievously played.

In quiet talks with his closest friends he confessed that he had not achieved his great purpose. Why? Because he was not privy to Administration plans and policies. He was not consulted on its programs, nor was his advice and counsel sought. His was the job of coming in to repair, as best he could, the damage after it had been created by some announcement or action, rather than that of preventing the debacle by prior consultation. He was not advised of or consulted upon the Henry Wallace or Aubrey Williams appointments; he was given no notice of the secret agreement at Yalta whereby Russia would ask and receive support for three votes in the Assembly of Nations. He did not know what was in the President's mind, or his advisers'. He knew nothing of the secrets of policy, nor was he consulted before arrangements were consummated. The voting arrangement concluded at Yalta raised an uproar in the Senate and deeply disturbed Senator Vandenberg whose co-operation and support were conceded to be essential to ratification of any treaty concluded for the future maintenance of peace. Truman was as surprised as anyone else, not excepting the Secretary of State, Edward R. Stettinius, Jr., who had come away from Yalta apparently with no knowledge of this secret arrangement between Roosevelt, Stalin and Churchill. But Truman defended the agreement to other Senators and did his level best to argue down the misgivings with which they received the surprising disclosure.

He was not given the opportunity to explain, because no explanations or intelligences were communicated to him. He was deprived of the opportunity to prevent clashes because his advice was not sought in advance. The nearly three months of being Vice-President were, for Truman, not exactly happy or rich with accomplishment. But the fault was not his.

It was on Wednesday afternoon, April 11, that he was chatting with a group of newsmen in the front of the Senate immediately after adjournment. They were twitting him about his office, and calling him, "Mr. President."

"Boys," said Truman, "those are fighting words out in Missouri where I came from. You'd better smile when you say that! You know right here is where I've always wanted to be, and the only place I ever wanted to be. The Senate —that's just my speed and my style."

Chapter Fourteen

The President

THE HANDS OF THE BLACK CLOCK STANDING ON THE mantel over the marble fireplace in Speaker Rayburn's "Board of Education" office pointed at ten after five on the afternoon of April 12, 1945. There were three men in the room: Speaker Rayburn; Lewis Deschler, the parliamentarian of the House of Representatives; and James Barnes, a sandy-haired man whom President Roosevelt had chosen as one of his executive assistants following Barnes's defeat for re-election to Congress in 1942.

The Speaker's private "Board of Education" room is tucked away at the southern end of the Capitol Building, being a comfortable room, but gloomy in some respects. Little light is admitted through the windows. Decorations and colors are almost entirely absent, and the faded flower design on the rug is frayed and worn thin.

One wall of the room comprises glassed-in book cupboards without books. Instead, the Speaker has filled the cases with unframed photographs, autographed for him by members of Congress. In front of these cabinets stands a plain mahogany desk and to the left a nook with a washbasin, running water, and face towels. Near by is a small electric refrigerator.

A wide, black leather couch and six leather-upholstered easy chairs are placed around informally; a tall mirror hangs over the fireplace above the clock. And in a niche at the opposite end of the room, hangs an oil painting of the Speaker, lighted by a special lamp. The kindly eyes of the portrait seem to take in every movement in the room.

The telephone on the desk rang abruptly and Deschler said he would answer, but Speaker Rayburn took the call. It was White House Secretary Stephen T. Early asking for the Vice-President. Early had just telephoned the Vice-President's office and learned that Truman was on his way to Rayburn's "Board of Education" to pay an unofficial call. Early's voice sounded strained and agitated.

Almost as Rayburn replaced the receiver after promising Early to have the Vice-President return the call, Harry Truman stepped into the room. He was wearing a double-breasted gray suit with his bronze army discharge pin in the left lapel. The folds of his bow tie were neatly in place.

"Hello, Sam," he grinned and likewise greeted the other two men.

He was about to sit down in one of the comfortable leather chairs when Rayburn advised him of the White House call.

"I'll get them for you, Harry," the Speaker said.

"No, I'll do it." Truman smiled as he picked up the telephone and asked for the White House. He got Early and said, "This is the Vice-President." The others in the room sat quietly while Truman listened intently, said abruptly, "All right," and then hung up. As he turned away from the telephone there was a noticeable trace of anxiety in his countenance. His face turned pale. Drawing a deep breath he suddenly blurted out, "Holy General Jackson: Steve Early wants me at the White House immediately!"

Then, recovering his composure, he said, half in a whisper, "Boys, this is in the room. Keep this quiet. Something must have happened."

Speaker Rayburn had laid down his cigarette in a glass ash receiver. Smoke twisted and curled upward toward the ceiling almost enveloping the silence in the room.

The Capitol was practically deserted and no sounds came in from the corridors outside—just a moment of utter stillness made eloquent only by the thoughts of the four men in the room. Each was thinking the same thing but dared not speak it.

"I'll get your hat," Deschler said.

"I left it over at my office. I'll get it there," Truman replied as he stood at the door. His face was now nearly the color of chalk.

"Harry, we'll stand by you," Rayburn said feelingly.

"Good-by," said Truman gravely. In an instant he was gone.

It was only five-fifteen by the mantel clock when he closed the door and the latch clicked in the lock. A few minutes later, George Donovan, the Speaker's chauffeur,

The President

telephoned and said, "Mr. Rayburn, a newspaperman just told me—the President is dead!"

Within half an hour there was another call; this one from Harry Truman in the White House. He wanted the Speaker and other Congressional leaders to come at once. He had raced back to his office to get his hat, and then had been driven to the White House quietly and quickly in his official car. He went, as directed, to the sitting room of the big executive mansion; and there Mrs. Roosevelt, calm and completely in control of her feelings, had told him that the President had passed away.

"What can I do?" Truman asked simply.

"Tell us, what can we do to help you?" the tall woman asked firmly.

Word of the President's death was spreading like fire and within what seemed a matter of moments, a crowd of some three thousand had gathered in Lafayette Park directly across Pennsylvania Avenue from the White House. They stood and looked, shifting from one foot to another and talking in hushed tones. A woman sobbed. A child pointed at a squirrel jumping in the trees. The crowd kept staring at the familiar building across the street as if they could see what was happening inside.

In the mansion there was the wildest confusion as more than a hundred reporters raced and ran about for scraps of information, then hurried to the press room near the Executive Chambers to relay the news to their offices. Cameramen shoved through for positions of vantage. Newsreel and radio men strung and uncoiled wires and cable through the length of the lobby. The cabinet had met with the Vice-President. Chief Justice Harlan Fiske Stone was on his way to administer the Presidential oath. Members of Congress were hurrying in. Some of the cabinet men had broken down and were openly weeping. Bess Truman and Mary Margaret were coming to witness the oath taking. Cabinet members had offered their resignations but Truman had asked them all to stay on for the present.

After two frantic hours, at exactly 7:09 P.M. in the presence of the grief-stricken cabinet and leaders of Congress, Chief Justice Stone, in a plain dark suit, lifted up a Bible which had been hastily brought from one of the White House offices, held up his right hand and solemnly administered the oath of the President of the United States. Truman repeated the words with his hand placed firmly on the Holy Book.

The heaviest of all loads, the insufferable burden that tires and kills even as it confers honors and historical significance upon all who assume it, had fallen upon this quiet, plain-spoken man who thirty years before had imagined for himself the life of a Missouri farmer.

Eleanor Roosevelt immediately left by plane for Warm Springs, Georgia, to accompany the President's body on the long funeral train back to Washington and then to Hyde Park where the grave was already being prepared at the ancestral estate. The body would not lie in state.

The swearing in of Harry S. Truman as the thirty-second

The President

President of the United States was a tense and strained occasion. But after Truman had taken the oath and shaken hands with Chief Justice Stone, the United States had a President whose motto had long been, "It's what you learn after you know it all, that counts."

He is a man poured evenly into the mold of the American people. A small-town boy born in modest circumstances, then a drugstore helper at three dollars a week, then newsboy, railroad hand, bank clerk, farmer, soldier, manager of a clothing store that failed, county judge, Senator and chairman of an important Senate committee, Vice-President, and finally President of the United States. There had been no social or economic barriers nor revolutionary upheavals. Lack of wealth, privilege, or a college education had made no difference. It was the precise pattern of the American success story. Little Johnny Jones living down the block in the brick house—he could be President some day. And so could Jimmy Smith who works after school delivering grocery orders. It had all been a perfectly natural and orderly process. And there he was—an ordinary common-sense citizen occupying the nation's highest office. In more than a century and a half of American history the same thing had happened many times.

The only peculiarity was that to Harry Truman's way of thinking, his arrival came by accident and not from choice. He had not sought the office nor strived for it. Yet his mind and heart were as one with the ideas and ideals of the people, and this gave him the strength to shoulder the bur-

The President

den. His approach to the Presidency might be expressed in the words of former Chief Justice Charles Evans Hughes who said in addressing an anniversary meeting of Congress with the executive and judicial branches of government:

We are not here as masters, but as servants, not to glory in power, but to attest our loyalty to the commands and restrictions laid down by our sovereign, the people of the United States, in whose name and by whose will we exercise our brief authority.

John Nance Garner of Texas had often made the sage observation that the United States did not want a brilliant President or need one, for such a man would get too far ahead of the country. In Harry Truman, the people have a President who claims no brilliance, who recognizes his own limitations and those of his people and from that very fact derives the capacity to lead. By depreciating his own worth and in his earnest desire to give the other man the benefit of doubts, he understands clearly and can closely gauge the will of the majority, and the rights of the few.

But there were burning questions that night of April 12, 1945, that flared brightly and ominously. Can Harry Truman measure up to the Presidency? What did this sudden though simple fact of death mean to America? Could it survive such a staggering shock in the midst of world conflict? The buoyant force of Franklin Roosevelt had almost completely dwarfed and obscured the qualities that reposed in his successor to office. And Harry Truman discounted

Truman enjoys rare moments of relaxation at the piano. He plays by note and prefers classical music. Here he is shown sitting at the keyboard in Washington while he was Vice-president of the United States.

Press Association, Inc.

One of the most intensely dramatic scenes ever recorded by camera. On April 12, 1945, at 7:05 P.M., Harry S. Truman is sworn in at the White House as President of the United States. Standing, left to right: Labor Secretary Frances Perkins, War Secretary Henry Stimson, Commerce Secretary Henry A. Wallace, War Production Board Chief J. A. Krug, Navy Secretary James Forrestal, Agriculture Secretary Claude Wickard, Unidentified, Attorney General Francis Biddle, Truman, Secretary of State Edward R. Stettinius, Jr., Mrs. Truman, Interior Secretary Harold L. Ickes, Chief Justice Harlan F. Stone, Speaker of the House Sam Rayburn, War Mobilizer Fred M. Vinson, and Congressmen Joseph Martin, Robert Ramspeck, and John McCormick.

himself. That had always been part of his success. It could also mean his failure if the people now discounted him.

So-called personalized government had reached a high level of expression under President Roosevelt, a situation that the public sensed but did not fully comprehend. Under ordinary circumstances even an unusually brilliant man entering upon the Presidency from the Vice-Presidency does so with considerable lack of information regarding official policy, departmental affairs, and the countless problems and arrangements peculiar to the executive branch. Personalized government tends to magnify and aggravate this handicap. Under Roosevelt it had reached a point where the task thrust upon Harry Truman was made inordinately difficult and complex. War was flaming on two fronts and the world was writhing under the impact of revolutionary forces that no man could yet fully understand. Casualty lists were reaching appalling totals. And only the framework of an international peace plan had been formed. Roosevelt had led the nation within sight of victory. But he had largely served as his own cabinet. His policies were those he had evolved himself with the reasons known mostly only to him. There was no group of men in government who could be called in to give the new President the intimate details nor even the general background essential to a thorough understanding of the immediate problems faced by the man occupying the President's chair at that moment.

On the day of Franklin Roosevelt's death, Edward J. Flynn, a political leader in New York State, was on a

The President

delicate, private diplomatic mission for the President, apparently seeking to arrange some rapprochement between Soviet Russia and the Vatican. Only he and the deceased President knew the instructions and the duties he was to perform under them.

Myron C. Taylor, President Roosevelt's personal envoy to the Vatican, occupied a similar status. Judge Samuel I. Rosenman was in Europe on a special food mission for the dead President. Ambassador Patrick J. Hurley was in Moscow dealing with the Soviet Union after completing conferences in London while en route back to his post in Chungking, China.

Hurley's mission also was highly confidential. For months he had been striving ineffectually to bring some area of agreement between China's central government as represented by Chiang Kai-shek and the Communist groups. Much depended on the attitude that Russia would take in this dispute, and whether Josef Stalin would interest himself actively in behalf of the Communists. Hurley, operating under special instructions of the President, alone knew the full purview of his authority and the extent of the propositions he was warranted to make as a representative of President Roosevelt.

Harry Hopkins lay ill at the Mayo clinic in Rochester, Minnesota. He had acted as Mr. Roosevelt's confidant and adviser for, many believed, too many years. No one, including the Department of State, knew what other arrangements may have been concluded at Yalta between Roosevelt,

The President

Stalin and Churchill. The secret agreement to support the Russian claim for three votes in the Assembly of Nations, when disclosed, came as a shock and a warning that still other undisclosed bargains may have been struck. President Truman could not and did not know anything about these arrangements. The Administration, as he had complained, had made little effort to take him into its confidence. He saw Roosevelt infrequently and on such occasions the discussion seldom involved the more important matters of world policy and high governmental affairs.

Such realizations as these caused apprehension on the night of Franklin Roosevelt's death. It was felt that Truman in his emergence from comparative obscurity had to set out upon his task like a man groping in an unlighted corridor between two dark rooms. In many ways the very future of the world depended upon what he did. And he was not trained to think in cosmic terms. He lacked the inspiring touch and the flair for dealing in vast schemes and philosophies of global government.

Fears in the night of Roosevelt's passing were founded on ignorance not merely of one man but of 139 million people and their form of government. Actually, Harry Truman had only to set out and prove what had often been demonstrated in the past—that the American people are capable of wise and progressive self-government. They function best when hampered least. The brilliant victories of American armies in the field of battle and the miracle of

The President

American war production resulted from the exercise of the collective wits of many, not from the brains of a few.

Consequently Truman's accession to the Presidency places squarely upon the people and their chosen representatives in Congress a heavy responsibility. This they have already sensed. Moreover it is apparent that Harry Truman is well qualified to be President, as Roosevelt himself thoroughly understood. However, co-operation and support will insure his success. Skepticism and thoughtless criticism can only serve to hamper his efforts.

In Congress there are other men like Harry Truman. For many years he was included in the more representative and progressive elements in the United States Senate. Their problems were also his problems. Together they were guided by much the same motives and thought generally along similar lines. Working together again, Truman freely predicts that he can give the country a stable and constructive administration.

The very nature and character of the new President will tend to eliminate bitter factional strife. Truman pledged himself to carry out the policies of Roosevelt and this he will do wherever the course is clearly charted. When the objectives become blurred and indistinct, he will strike out on his own with inclinations that allow free play of the checks and balances of the constitutional system. Since he is not bound nor influenced by the various minority pressure groups, he need not nourish inherited political controversies. His political acumen and wide experience in public affairs

The President

will help him tread carefully, avoiding the arena of the more radical elements, while also revising the policies which the Republicans so bitterly complained of during the "twelve long years" under Roosevelt. Harry Truman can be counted on to stretch and staple his political fences as expertly as he wired in the pasture lands out on the farm.

Truman can provide stability and continuity of foreign policy. He need not try to sweep all the corners clean at once and can rely on the counsel of many men designated by Roosevelt who have great knowledge and understanding of foreign governments. Truman has no campaign obligations and so can make his changes quietly and deliberately. Moreover, with the help of a Congress which he knows and understands, a more realistic approach can be smoothly effected.

His own personal lack of knowledge in foreign affairs he has already largely overcome. Being President he has access to exclusive sources of information. His broad understanding of history and the long service he saw in the United States Senate, particularly as chairman of the Truman Committee, provide him with the most specialized type of experience.

Truman is averse to "palace politics" and believes in appointments made under statutory grants of authority with the duties clearly set forth. He views with suspicion those advisers who operate outside the scope of established office. He picks able men and upholds them. If they fail, he favors their replacement.

The President

However, since Truman came into the White House along the loyal party campaign route, thousands who can claim they supported him will descend upon Washington in search of special favors. Conniving coteries and cabals sprout like weeds in the atmosphere of immense power embodying the Office of the President. The authority to confer favors and honors carries within it a tendency to make mistakes. Not everyone by any means visits the White House with sincere and altruistic purposes. Too often there are selfish, greedy, or dishonest motives involved. Ugly scandal can result if private desires are not thoroughly understood and accurately appraised with favors conferred only within proper limits. Truman is well aware of this source of evil and so far has successfully avoided stepping into the pitfall.

In the final analysis, the trend of world events will largely shape the acts of the Truman Administration. From the swift currents of war and the whirlpools of economic upheaval flow the changes that will determine the course of America's future destiny. Harry Truman is confident as this destiny approaches. He has often observed, "Not everything in war is on the debit side. War does not permit going back to the old way of doing things. . . . It shakes our very foundations, but what is best in them is so obviously right and needed that it is strong enough to survive. . . . In peacetime it is easy to do business at the old stand in the time-honored way . . . and to follow the old maxim of 'let well enough alone.'

"America has a great future after the war . . . a pros-

The President

perity beyond anything we have ever had before is available
to us. . . . If we fail the failure will be due to ourselves
and not to our lack of opportunity."

In the quiet of meditation, Harry Truman can also reflect upon his own destiny. Perhaps his voice will even say,
'This is just where I want to be—here in the White House
as President of the United States.' He has to learn his job
the hard way but that has always been part of his life. His
confidence in himself was expressed in the words he spoke
so devoutly in his first address to Congress: "I ask only
to be a good and faithful servant of my Lord and my
people."

THE END

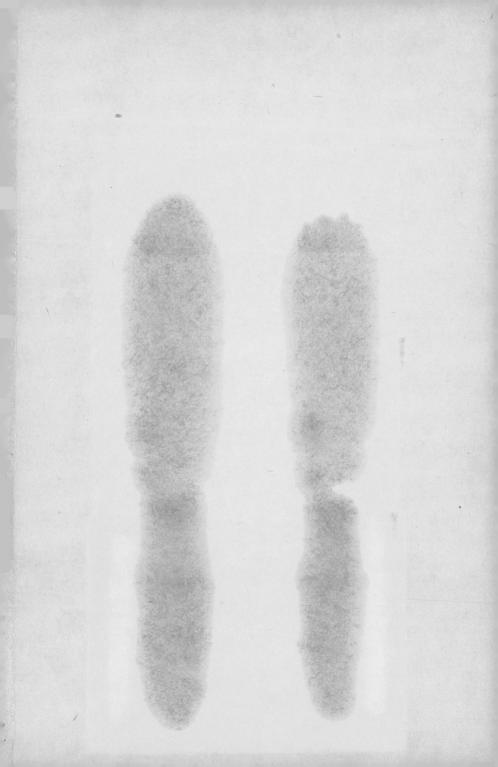